FUNRETROSPECTIVES

Editora Caroli
caroli.org

Editorial coordination
Juliana Rodrigues | Algo Novo Editorial

Proofreading
Laura Folgueira

Graphic design, layout and cover
Vanessa Lima

Copyright © 2020 by
Tainã Caetano Coimbra and Paulo Caroli
All the rights reserved to
Editora Caroli.
Avenida Itajai, 310 - Petrópolis
Porto Alegre, RS, Brasil - 90470-140
www.caroli.org/editora
contato@caroli.org

 PUBLISHER'S NOTE

Activities presented here by the authors were taught
to them throughout their professional careers.
Every effort has been made to find the right references
for these contents. If you, reader, know of any credit not presented
here, please contact us at contact@funretrospectives.com.

Cataloging-in-Publication Data (CIP)
Angelica Ilacqua CRB-8/7057

Caroli, Paulo
        Funretrospectives: activities and ideas for making agile retrospectives more
engaging / Paulo Caroli & Tainã Caetano Coimbra. - São Paulo: Editora Caroli, 2020.
        240 p. : il.

ISBN 978-65-86660-07-4

1. Meetings 2. Meetings - Techniques 3. Teams in the workplace I. Title II. Coimbra, Tainã
Caetano

20-2394   CDD 658.456
                            Index for Systematic Catalog:
                                    1. Meetings

PAULO CAROLI & TAINÃ CAETANO COIMBRA

FUNRETROSPECTIVES

ACTIVITIES AND IDEAS FOR MAKING AGILE RETROSPECTIVES MORE ENGAGING

Editora
Caroli
caroli.org

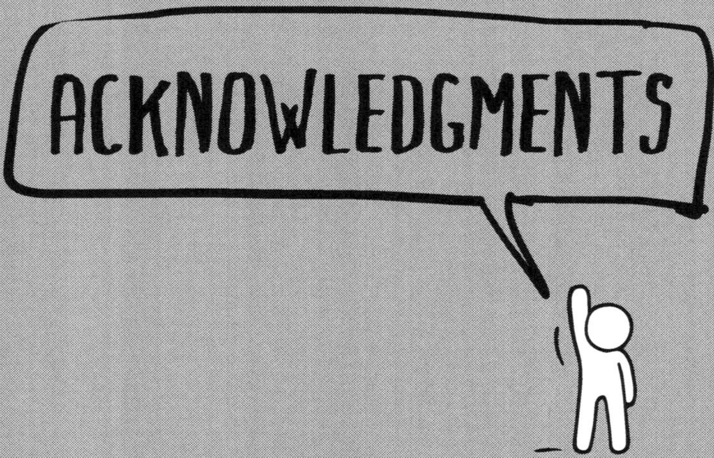
ACKNOWLEDGMENTS

We thank the entire agile community for being a part of this book. The recommendations, comments, and feedback were essential for improving the content. We thank each and every one who shared their ideas, suggestions, and activities with us. Amongst the many enthusiasts with whom we worked, we would like to thank Alejandro Olchik, Bethlem Migot, Bill Kimmel, Charles Du, David Worthington, Diana Larsen, Fabio Pereira, Felipe Carvalho, Fernando Carlini Guimarães, Gabriel Albo, Heitor Roriz, Luiz Lula Rodrigues, Marcos Garrido, Mayra Souza, Patrick Kua, Rafael Ferreira, Rafael Sabbagh, Samuel Cavalcante, Silvio Meira, Steve Wells, Verônica Rodrigues Moschetta, and Vinicius Gomes.

Thank you to all the people and the many teams with whom we have worked. Our time working and learning together is what motivated us to write and share the knowledge and experiences in this book.

Thank you to ThoughtWorks for its leadership in the agile community and for its attitude in regard to respect, diversity, and people development. Thank you to Split for fostering learning and continuous improvement, and for empowering teams to be successful.

Finally, we thank our dear family and friends, who are always there to support us every day. Without you, none of this would have been possible.

INDEX

FOREWORD 10

PRESENTATION 14
How This Book Was Created 15
What You Will Find Here 16

ALL YOU NEED TO KNOW BEFORE YOUR FUNRETRO 18
Why are FunRetros so Important? 19
Planning is Essencial 20
The 7 Steps Agenda 22
Think About Columns and Colors 29
Remote Retrospectives 32

ACTIVITIES CATALOG 34

ENERGIZERS 37
Punctual Paulo 📶* 38
Fun Fact 📶 40
Geographic Location 📶 42
Visual Phone 44
One Two Ping Four Pong 📶 46
Peer Introduction Game 📶 48
Cardinal Directions 📶 50
Forming Triangles 54
Zip-zap-zoom 📶 56
Balloon Battle 58
Untangle Yourselfs 60
Complex Pieces 62

*📶 Activities that work well for remote teams.

Back to Back 63
Find your Peers 65
Collaborative Face Drawing 66
Human Rock-Paper-Scissors 🛜 68

CHECK-IN 70
Safety Check 🛜 71
ESVP: Explorer, Shopper, Vacationer, Prisoner 🛜 ... 74
Happiness Radar 🛜 76
Happiness Radar for a Timeline 🛜 78
One Word 🛜 80
Anonymous Note 🛜 82
Draw your Feelings 🛜 84

MAIN COURSE: TEAM BUILDING 86
Defining the Team Vision Statement 🛜 87
The Team Is - Is Not - Does - Does Not 🛜 89
Understanding the Group Knowledge 🛜 91
Creating Safety 🛜 94
360 Degrees Appreciation 🛜 96
General Behavior Activity 🛜 98
That Person & This Person 🛜 100
Trade-off Sliders 🛜 102
Role Expectations Matrix 🛜 104
Delegation Map 🛜 106
Ground Rules 🛜 109
Defining the Team Principles 🛜 111
Candy love 113
Roles We Play 🛜 115
SWOT - Strengths, Weaknesses, Opportunities, Threats 🛜 ... 117

MAIN COURSE: RETROSPECTIVES, LOOKING BACK ... 119
Well, Not So Well, New Ideas 🛜 120
Peaks and Valleys Timeline 🛜 122

Empathy Snap on Big Hitter Moments 📶 124

Repeat/Avoid 📶 126

Speed Car 📶 127

Hot-air Balloon 📶 128

Anchors and Engine 📶 130

WWW: Worked Well, Kinda Worked, Didn't Work 📶 132

KALM - Keep, Add, More, Less 📶 134

Open the Box 📶 136

The Story of a Story 📶 138

Known Issues 📶 140

Problems & Actions 📶 142

Thumbs Up, Thumbs Down, New Ideas and Acknowledgement 📶 144

Timeline Driven by Feelings 📶 146

Timeline Driven by Data 📶 148

Future Direction, Lessons Learned,
Accomplishments and Problem Areas (FLAP) 📶 150

Dealing with Failure - FMEA 📶 152

DAKI - Drop, Add, Keep, Improve 📶 154

The 3Ls: Liked, Learned, Lacked 📶 156

Starfish 📶 158

Lessons Learned - Planned vs. Success 📶 160

Pleasure and Gain 📶 162

Three Little Pigs 📶 164

Error Conversation 📶 166

MAIN COURSE: FUTURESPECTIVES, LOOKING AHEAD

MAIN COURSE: FUTURESPECTIVES, LOOKING AHEAD 168

Hopes and Concerns 📶 169

Plan of Action 📶 171

Path to Nirvana 📶 173

Pre-Mortem Activity 📶 176

Speed Car - Abyss 📶 178

Hot-air Balloon - Bad Weather 📶 180

Future Facebook Posts 📶 182

PMI - Plus, Minus, Interesting 📶 184

Risk Brainstorming and Mitigation 📶 186
Letters to the Future 📶 188
RAID - Risks, Assumptions, Issues and Dependencies 📶 190
The Catapult 📶 192
Success Criteria 📶 194
Hero's Journey 📶 196

FILTERING 198

Dot Voting 📶 199
Select One and Talk 📶 201
Plus Minus Voting 📶 203
Tell and Cluster 📶 205
Fishbowl Conversation 📶 207
Feasible x Useful 📶 209
Likelihood x Impact 📶 211
Effort x Pain 📶 213

CHECK-OUT 215

Who-What-When Steps to Action 📶 216
Following Up on Action Items 📶 218
SMART Items 📶 220
Feedback and ROI 📶 222
Token of Appreciation 📶 224
Learning Scale 📶 226
Note to Self 📶 228
One Word Before Leaving 📶 230
Fun Photo 📶 232

THANKS FOR READING 234
WHERE TO FIND MORE 236
JOIN THE FUNRETROSPECTIVES TRAINING 237
ABOUT THE AUTHORS 238
ABOUT EDITORA CAROLI 239

FOREWORD

My team doesn't want to hold retrospectives anymore."

"Our retros are a boring waste of time."

As a coach/facilitator and co-author of *Agile Retrospectives: Making Good Teams Great*, I'm a proponent of effective team processes. I participate in forums and communities devoted to helping teams become their best. I get invited to speak and attend events all around the globe.

Wherever I go, I hear: "My team doesn't want to hold retrospectives anymore. They say they are a boring waste of time. What can I do?" If I had a penny (as the saying goes) for every time I've heard this complaint, I would be a wealthy woman. Hearing this makes me sad, because it can only mean a few things.

First, it could mean that the team leader (whether scrum master, agile coach, tech lead or manager) gave in to the team's request and stopped making time for retrospective collaboration. This is disappointing. It takes away an opportunity for the team to reach greatness through learning and improvement actions.

Second, it could mean that the team sees no point in "reflect, tune, and adjust" because they get no support for the improvement actions and experiments that they attempt. Organizational antibodies shut down team efforts. The team hasn't examined its options to advocate for itself. Discouraging.

Third, it could also mean that the team leader has continued to deliver those boring wastes of time disguised as Important Meetings. Which is boring and wastes everyone's time! (Pro tip: Don't do that!)

Often, I ask the person questioning me to tell me more about the situation. Their stories are how I know about the three behavior patterns above. I commiserate. Then I get curious about how this leader is, or isn't, fostering a culture of learning with their team. I may share the "Five Rules of Accelerated Learning"[1] and suggest ways enlivening the retrospective session.

Lively, focused retrospectives stand a greater chance of effective outcomes. So I frequently offer the link to funretrospectives. com as a great source of ways to perk up team members and the event as a whole.

I'm delighted that Paulo and TC have decided to pull all their ideas for improving retrospectives into one place: this book! Now I have a handy answer to the inevitable question. I can recommend this book. I'll say: "It will give you guidance for designing your retros, along with an extensive catalog of collaborative learning activities."

Many of these activities have been floating around team space for some time and their antecedents have been lost in the handoffs to handoffs to handoffs. They are old familiar friends to me, but may be quite new to you!

[1]   LARSEN, Willem; LARSEN, Diana. *The Five Rules of Accelerated Learning*. Leanpub, 2019.

As Paulo and TC suggest, first consider your teams—their circumstances, history, and context. Then browse through the activities to put together a retrospective flow that will energize, engage, and improve team outcomes.

That conversation I mentioned above usually ends the same way I will conclude this preface: I wish you the best of luck with all your future retrospectives. And know that this book can help.

Diana Larsen
coach, facilitator, co-author of the book *Agile Retrospectives: Making Good Teams Great* and co-founder of www.agilefluency.org.

PRESENTATION

HOW THIS BOOK WAS CREATED

Since 2013, we have been collaborating with many supporters to talk about and share FunRetrospectives. We fostered this community and gathered the content through the website FunRetrospectives. com, the FunRetrospectives e-book, talks, and training.

But how did the "fun" part come about in retrospectives?

The name was suggested by Patrick Kua in 2013. Pat is our friend who is also author of the great *The Retrospective Handbook: A guide for agile teams*. While we were organizing retrospective activities in a new website dedicated especially to them, we met Pat when he was on a business trip in Brazil.

Then, we asked him: "We need a name for the website and the e-book that we are going to create. What do you suggest?" Pat replied: "Caroli, you make retrospectives lighter, you have a different style. Your activities are more… fun!"

And it was from this conversation that the name FunRetrospectives came up and, after that, the nickname "FunRetro."

Retro is short for retrospective. It was already common for people to say "let's do a retro," instead of saying 'let's do a retrospective."

As many people were using the FunRetrospectives activities, they started to say: "Let's do a FunRetro!"

WHAT YOU WILL FIND HERE

This book helps you with two things: one, planning and structuring your retrospective agenda; and two, provide you with lots of activities and ideas. As such, you can use it as a quick reading to improve your understanding of retrospectives, with new ideas for your meetings; and as a handy catalog to browse when you need to choose an activity for your upcoming retrospective.

We strongly recommend reading the chapter "All You Need to Know Before Your FunRetro" first to better understand the agenda structure, different types of activities, and how to connect them. After that, the catalog is a quick reference for when you need to choose one activity to use.

We start by introducing the seven steps agenda, with a structure on how to think about, prepare, and organize the meeting. By analyzing the team's context and where they're at, you'll be equipped to choose the best set of activities to use.

We then follow with a catalog of different types of activities. All activities follow a pattern about its classification, a simple step-by-step on how to run it, as well as tips and advice for adapting to remote meetings.

This extensive catalog is based on years of experience by us and our colleagues, being a collaborative effort from the retrospective community. We thank each and every one of the community members who have shared their knowledge and helped us build this catalog.

This is a complementary book that works well in conjunction with other books about retrospectives and facilitation. We strongly recommend books by the author of our foreword and other amazing people like her, who deepen the knowledge on the subject and explore different aspects of facilitation, team bonding, and team dynamics.

ALL YOU NEED TO KNOW BEFORE YOUR FUNRETRO

WHY ARE FUNRETROS SO IMPORTANT?

A team is a group of people focused on a common goal, in which each individual adjusts their actions, habits, and work preferences in order to achieve the group's common goal. The team's effectiveness depends on the members' capacity to work together. It is directly related to the group's ability to make the best use of the individuals' skills.

However, a group of people does not turn into a team overnight. It takes time to create bonds between colleagues, and this time can be shortened with the appropriate setting. As the team progresses after its formation, team members may face moments in which they will want to reflect and analyze the past or imagine and prepare for the future. These moments may be recurring, and keeping the enthusiasm is the key for maintaining the team effective. Over time, the group will tune up its ability to work together. Group's disagreements will be discussed. Individual capabilities will rise up. The group will continuously seek the best balance for everyone's contribution toward a common goal. Collectively, the team will improve.

How to transform a group of people into an effective team? Keeping participants amused and providing a setting where they can reflect, discuss, and have fun is key to continuous improvement. In this book, we provide you a toolset of activities to achieve this!

The catalog presented here is composed by a set of activities, each one appropriate for different contexts and teams:

* **Energizers:** activities to start off any meeting and get people energized.
* **Check-in:** activities to measure participants' engagement and understand more about their feelings at the start of a meeting.
* **Team building:** activities to define ground rules and get a team started.
* **Retrospectives:** activities to look back and reflect on the past.
* **Futurespectives:** activities to look ahead and plan for the future.
* **Filtering:** activities to prioritize items for discussion.
* **Check-out:** activities to organize action items or collect feedback about the meeting.

PLANNING IS ESSENTIAL

The retrospective is a meeting that usually lasts one hour, happening periodically (once a week or once a sprint for Scrum teams, for instance), in which team members talk about what was good in that period, what could be improved and what should be done to improve it.

It is essential to unite the team towards a common goal and to avoid misunderstandings becoming interpersonal issues within the team, which would lead to even less communication and eventually to the group's rupture. The retrospective also fosters an environment in which people listen to each other's feelings and reflect, talking about specific subjects (related to the context and the team's moment), and looking for Kaizen—the continuous improvement.

Here are some factors you should look at when planning your retrospective:

→ **MOMENT –** Where are you in the timeline? Are you in the very beginning of a team? Are you trying to learn with the past? Are you preparing for an upcoming event or release?

→ **CONTEXT –** What are you looking for? Are you seeking focused action items? Do you need to increase the team's morale? Do you need time for acknowledgement? Do you want to get a measure of the team's progress and/or happiness?

Based on those factors, you need to choose what activity (or sequence of activities) is more appropriate to use. Besides thinking about the best retrospective for a given moment and context, it is important to keep in mind that many teams have the retrospective as a recurring meeting. As such, they look for alternatives to avoid the monotony caused by the repetition of the same agenda and activities over and over again. When you change it a little bit and present new activities, the team can look through different angles and perspectives, generating new insights.

THE 7 STEPS AGENDA

This book gives you a toolset with many ideas and activities. Those activities can be used individually in different contexts. In many instances, however, we use them in the context of a team meeting. For instance, the recurring Scrum[2] retrospective is a meeting in which a sequence of activities is applied.

Be it a Scrum retrospective meeting, a meeting about project risks or even a project kick-off meeting, we use and strongly suggest the following agenda structure. This agenda outlines the seven steps that you will be taking to achieve your goal:

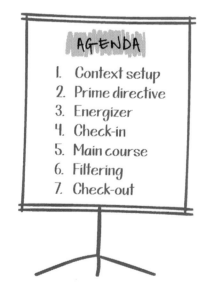

AGENDA

1. Context setup
2. Prime directive
3. Energizer
4. Check-in
5. Main course
6. Filtering
7. Check-out

CONTEXT SETUP

Setting the context at the beginning of any meeting is the first step you can take to ensure that the meeting is effective. Participants need to understand what the focus of the meeting is.

---

[2]   SCHWABER, Ken; BEEDLE, Mike. *Agile Software Development with Scrum*. Pearson, 2001.

You either start the meeting with a well-defined context and share it with the team, or you define it in real time with participants, asking: "So, what is the context for this retrospective?"

Below are some sample contexts:

→ "This retrospective is a bi-weekly recurring Scrum retrospective for the ABC team. We are on the Sprint 12 out of 30."

→ "In 14 days, our artifact should reach the main production stage."

→ "Feature XYZ failed bad, bringing the servers down for two hours until sys-admin could bring the older version back up."

→ 'This team will work together in a new project starting today.'

→ "We have worked together in the past year. We will be working together for another year to come."

→ "This diverse group of people has participated in the BI-ZANK event. Most likely another group of people from our company will take part in similar future events. What should we share with them?"

→ "We delivered the planned features on schedule. Let's discuss what were the factors that helped us to be successful."

By setting the context, you are not only aligning the participants towards a common goal. You are also narrowing down the discussion for the steps that will follow.

PRIME DIRECTIVE

In Project Retrospectives,[3] Kerth introduced the prime directive, a statement that intended to help set the stage for the retrospective.

> *"Regardless of what we discover, we understand and truly believe that everyone did the best job they could, given what was known at the time, their skills and abilities, the resources available, and the situation at hand."*

The Prime Directive is a statement that helps drive people into a collaborative mindset. It's a belief that the team must hold during the activities to follow. More than that, it sets the stage for the expected attitude during the meeting.

Kerth's prime directive is appropriate for retrospectives, but it can be changed as needed to fit other kinds of activities. We suggest the following directive for meetings in which you will run team building activities:

> *"Cooperation is the act of working with others and acting together to accomplish a job. A team is a partnership of unique people who bring out the very best in each other, and who know that even though they are wonderful as individuals, they are even better together. Coming together is a beginning; staying together is progress; working together is success."*

[3]   KERTH, Norman. *Project Retrospectives: A Handbook for Team Reviews*. Dorset House, 2001.

The following directive is recommended to set the stage for futurespectives, meetings where the team will look ahead and plan for the future:

"Hope and confidence come from proper involvement and a willingness to predict the unpredictable. We will fully engage in this opportunity to unite around an inclusive vision and join hands in constructing a shared future."

We recommend reading the appropriate prime directive out loud for the team before starting the planned activities, as well as keeping it visible while the meeting happens. You can always reference it to remember participants that, for this meeting, the team should put judgments aside.

ENERGIZER

The energizer, also known as icebreaker, is an activity to warm up the team and promote group interaction. It is a good starter for any team meeting and extra valuable for early stages of team building.

You should select an energizer activity to match the needs of your team meeting. When forming a new team, we recommend activities that focus on sharing information, such as names and hobbies. When morale is low, choose activities that bring happiness and fun to the group.

This kind of activity helps to create a friendly environment and make people more comfortable to take part in the activities that will follow.

Some examples of activities are Zip-Zap-Zoom, Fun Fact, and Untangle Yourselves.

CHECK-IN

Check-in activities gather information such as how participants feel toward the meeting and how they feel regarding the given context. It is also a good step to narrow down the themes that will be discussed in the meeting.

Another benefit of doing a check-in is that it helps people put aside their concerns and then focus on the meeting at hand. Depending on the activity, it also works for helping participants put aside their judgments at least for the duration of the meeting.

These are usually short activities. Think of them as a quick bite to open everyone's appetite for the main course. It gives participants a feeling for the next activity, while giving you feedback about participants' engagement.

Safety Check, Happiness Radar, and One Word are some examples of check-in activities.

MAIN COURSE

The main course is the core of the meeting, and its goal is continuous improvement. It is composed of one or more activities and it is also the moment for the team to discuss their notes. These activities are used to gather data, bring up feelings, talk about the positive stuff, acknowledge people, and seek improvements. They drive the team to think about the given context, reinforce a shared vision and generate insights.

Teams that have retrospective as a recurring meeting will typically look for main course alternatives. By varying the activity, the team can look at different angles and perspectives, therefore generating new insights.

The main course is the moment for team members to feel heard. Some notes are discussed in detail, and all of them are visible to the whole team. Each and every individual note is acknowledged.

Choose your main course wisely, keeping the moment and context in mind. This is the main activity of your meeting, and most likely the information gathered and discussed will set the tone for continuous improvement.

Here are some examples: "Well, Not So Well, New Ideas," Open the Box, Path to Nirvana and Roles Expectation Matrix.

FILTERING

Filtering activities help focus the discussion. In many retrospectives, there isn't enough time to discuss all items brought up by the team. By prioritizing a number of select items and organizing the conversation, the team will be more effective in generating insights within the time they have.

In this book you will find options for filtering activities. For instance, the team may group notes based on similarity and then discuss the identified clusters. Another possibility is to vote and then focus on top-voted topics. Some examples are Dot Voting, Select One and Talk, and Tell and Cluster.

CHECK-OUT

You are about to leave a hotel after staying over a few nights. You want to do a check-out. You want it to be fast. But you were not alone at the hotel. You were with your teammates and, together, you had snacks, dinners, and other things that make up to the group's bill. How to split the bill? Who will pay for each of these items?

This is similar to what happens at the end of a retrospective: you might have many action items, and it is time to verify who will take which one. There are also times when the retrospective meeting wasn't just about actions; situations where the discussion itself was the main outcome, in which you still need some sort of check-out.

The check-out activity brings closure to the meeting. It is a fast activity that acknowledges what happened during the meeting, providing a structure for handling action items, to-do lists, or any other sort of generated artifact from your retrospective. These might lead to including new items to the team's backlog of work, e-mail the meeting notes to the organization, schedule another in-depth discussion about a specific item, among others.

Not all check-outs are about action items. Sometimes, the generated artifact is something as simple as a group picture that will be shared somewhere, or an individual anonymous note that each person will take home. The most important thing is: you must acknowledge what happened during the meeting and close it accordingly.

Who-What-When Steps to Action, Learning Scale, and Note to Self are some examples.

THINK ABOUT COLUMNS AND COLORS

When organizing your retrospective agenda, one key decision point is the main activity, the main course. At this decisive moment, you should think about the activity's columns and colors, as well as how to combine them to better suit your context and moment.

For instance, check the following three columns for a simple and common main course retrospective activity.

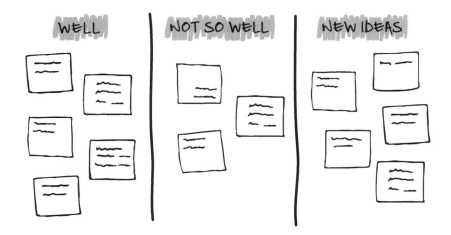

Participants in this retrospective meeting are asked to add notes to the board; they are being invited to think and express their points via written notes about: (1) What went well, (2) what did not go so well, and (3) new ideas, where (1) , (2) and (3) define specific areas to collect the data points and guide the conversation.

The activities catalog presents many options for activities, each of them with a specific format for collecting data points and guiding the conversation. The majority of them can be organized in just a few columns (or areas where people can add their notes).

Too many columns gets confusing, it's like asking: think about this and that, and that other thing, and that one as well, and one more... Bottomline, less is more. Less open options—less columns to think about—means more focused conversations and, typically, better results.

However, even in a well-defined activity with its few columns, the activity boundaries might be too wide. For instance, in the given sample context, what do you mean by what went well? What went well about what?

Do you mean: What went well about the people? About the environment? About the product? About the new payment flow? About the new hires? About the seniors? About the process? About the internal team? About the contractors? About the martial arts commanders? About the tools? About the technology? About the remote work? About the face-to-face work? About the Milky Way galaxy? About other galaxies?...

There can be so many different perspectives to look at these activities columns. You should not leave it widely open. While you want participants to express their thoughts and feelings, you must be clear about the perspectives on which you want to focus during this specific retrospective. Therefore, when building your retrospective agenda and thinking about the main course activity, you should also think about the different perspectives you want people to consider.

For instance, "in the context of our past two working weeks: what went well regarding the tools we have been using? What went well regarding the process we have been following? What went well regarding our people's interaction?"

In the same context, "what did not go so well regarding the tools we have been using? What did not go so well regarding the process we have been following? What did not go so well regarding our people's interaction?"

And still in this context, "do you have any new ideas for the tools we have been using? Do you have any new ideas for the process we have been following? Do you have any new ideas for our people's interaction?"

You can narrow down the focus of the meeting by asking leading questions, but with preparation you can do even better than that.

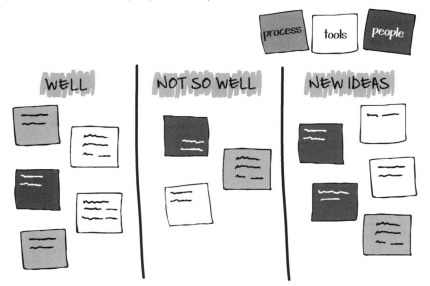

This is an example of when colors come into play. The columns define the boundaries for an activity, while the colors determine the different perspectives.

The combination of columns and colors is very powerful, combining context with boundaries and perspectives. Similarly to having too many columns, you should also avoid too many colors. Three colors typically give you enough perspectives to think about.

When building your retrospective agenda, consider the seven steps agenda and also think about how to combine your context with the activity columns and colors. This will help you push the team towards deeper, more valuable insights.

REMOTE RETROSPECTIVES

There is immeasurable value to human connection, therefore we must support effective interactions for both: local and remote retrospectives. We increasingly see a large amount of people using some sort of remote retrospective tool, given teams are getting more spread out by the day.

Many are the reasons to use a remote retrospective tool: working from home during the Coronavirus pandemic, staying close to your kids, avoiding traffic jams, working from the beach, using a reading device, dealing with work visa issues, working from a distant country etc.

Therefore, we invested time and effort on the App.FunRetrospectives. com, an online tool to help plan and facilitate remote retrospectives.

As we started sharing the online board, we realized that it was also useful when everyone is in the same room. Some teams were physically in the same place and still used the App.FunRetrospectives.com online board.

Here is a sample situation. The safety check is an anonymous activity to verify how safe people feel participating in the retrospective. Typically, we would ask everyone to use the same sticky note color and same pen color to write a number from 1 (not safe at all) to 5 (very safe to talk about anything) in the sticky note. We would collect it (using a bag or a hat) and the place on the board.

The online board is faster and safer (no one can recognize a hand writing)! We only had to share a link on the team messaging chat and verify the results.

So, we started using the online FunRetrospectives board even when we are running local retrospectives.

Having said that, please keep it light and fun. Even if your team is spread out, plan it accordingly and have a fun retrospective.

HAVE ONE RETROSPECTIVE PER WEEK, UNLESS YOU ARE TOO BUSY. IN THAT CASE, YOU SHOULD HAVE TWO!

ACTIVITIES CATALOG

In this catalog, you will find activities that are applicable in multiple scenarios. When planning your seven steps agenda, consider which activity (or set of activities) is better for the team's context and moment. By choosing activities tailored for a given situation, you will be able to engage people deeply and fully, while keeping the retrospective fun and effective.

More than that, having a variety of activities on your sleeve will help you avoid the monotony caused by the repetition of the same activities over and over again. Different activities will provide different angles and perspectives, which will allow the team to generate new insights.

Next to the activities' titles, you will see the  icon. It signals the ones that are easily adaptable for remote retrospectives. By the end of each of those activities, there is a board with some suggestions and tips to improve this adaptation. Unfortunately, some are very challenging to do remotely. But don't worry: since there are lots of options for variety, you can chose another one that fits the team's moment.

ENERGIZERS

Energizers are activities to warm up the team and to promote <u>group interaction</u>. It is a good starter for any team meeting and extra valuable for early stages of team building.

PUNCTUAL PAULO 📶

Punctual Paulo is a quick activity to help team members remember each other's names.

RUNNING THE ACTIVITY

1. Ask the participants to think about an adjective that begins with the same letter as their name.
2. Form a circle and ask each participant to say their name with the adjective, in turns. Fo exemplare: "Hi, I'm Punctual Paulo".
3. After all the participants speak, ask them to go clockwise telling the name and adjective for the person at their side.
4. After a few turns, ask the participants to repeat step 3 going counterclockwise.

Besides sharing some laughs and breaking the ice, this activity will also help the team associate people's names with an adjective, making it easier to remember them.

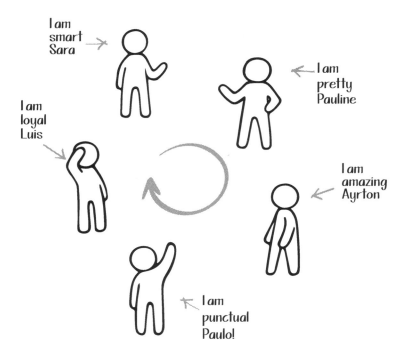

I am
smart
Sara

I am
pretty
Pauline

I am
loyal
Luis

I am
amazing
Ayrton

I am
punctual
Paulo!

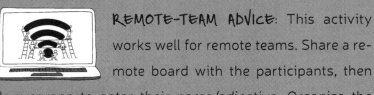

REMOTE-TEAM ADVICE: This activity works well for remote teams. Share a remote board with the participants, then ask everyone to enter their name/adjective. Organize the names in a sequence and follow it, asking each participant to say their name/adjective out loud. After the last name, go back to the first and repeat a few times.

FUN FACT 📶

Fun Fact is a simple and great energizer to get to know more about each other. People will anonymously write fun facts, then the group will try to match a person with their fun fact.

RUNNING THE ACTIVITY:

1. Ask the participants to think about a fun fact about themselves individually.
2. Instruct participants to write it on a note, anonymously.
3. Make all the fun facts visible to everyone.
4. Going one by one, let the group guess who the person is who wrote each fun fact.
5. Write the name of the person next to the fun fact.

This is a fast and fun activity. It is great to foster conversations and break the ice, so people get to know a little more about each other. A few examples: "I played in a punk-rock band", "I was a yoga teacher," "I'm a juggler."

FUN FACT

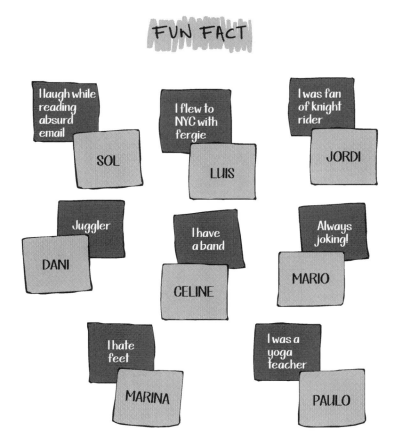

I laugh while reading absurd email

SOL

I flew to NYC with fergie

LUIS

I was fan of knight rider

JORDI

Juggler

DANI

I have a band

CELINE

Always joking!

MARIO

I hate feet

MARINA

I was a yoga teacher

PAULO

REMOTE-TEAM ADVICE: This activity works well for remote teams. Use the remote board of your choice.

GEOGRAPHIC LOCATION 📶

Geographic Location is a good ice-breaker and also helps team members to learn a little bit about each other.

RUNNING THE ACTIVITY:

1. Explain to participants that each one will be a geographic location (e.g.: their country, city or neighborhood).
2. Show where is north and south in the room.
3. Ask each participant to move to where they think they belong in order to create a map as close to scale as possible.
4. After everyone moves to their spot, ask one volunteer to draw a map representing the room.

This is a great activity to use when team members are still getting to know each other. It gives people something to talk about, like: "I didn't know you were born in Rio de Janeiro! How is it over there?". Collectively drawing brings unexpected and funny results.

REMOTE-TEAM ADVICE: This activity works well for remote teams. Share a remote board with participants, and ask them to enter their name and city in a sticky note. Instead of moving around, ask people to place their sticky note on the board.

VISUAL PHONE

Visual Phone is a great energizer to get everyone engaged while fostering a conversation about communication and its interpretations.

1. Break the large group into sets of three people (one or two groups can have four people).
2. Place three sticky notes and a pen in front of each person.
3. Ask everyone to write a sentence (on the sticky note), then place a blank sticky note on top of it (at this time, only the author of the sentence knows it).
4. Everyone passes the sticky note clockwise.
5. Each person reads the sentence from the sticky note in front of them, and then creates a representative drawing for the sentence (on the blank sticky note).
6. Everyone passes the sticky notes clockwise.
7. On a new sticky note, each person writes a sentence for the drawing in front of them, and places it on top of the sticky note set (now the set has three sticky notes: the original sentence, the drawing, and the new sentence).
8. Everyone passes the sticky note set clockwise (for the groups of three people, the set should end up in front of the original sentence writer).

9. Open the sticky note set so everyone can see the sentences and their respective drawings.

Typically, participants will laugh and have a great time comparing drawings and sentences.

This is a great energizer with a sublime message about communication (visual and written), context, and interpretations.

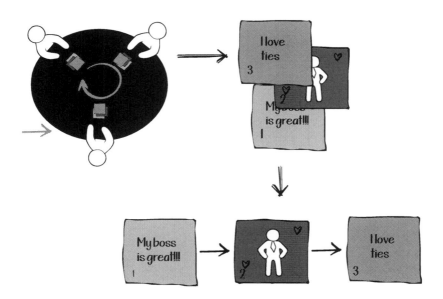

ONE TWO PING FOUR PONG 📶

One Two Ping Four Pong is a short activity to start up a meeting in a good mood and get participants engaged.

1. Ask participants to form a circle.
2. Participants must decide upon a direction to follow (clockwise or counterclockwise).
3. Someone starts by saying any positive number that is not a multiple of three or five.
4. The next person, following the agreed-upon direction, mentally increments the number by one. Then:
   * If the number is not a multiple of three or five: Says the number.
   * If the number is a multiple of three: Says ping and claps.
   * If the number is a multiple of five: Says pong and jumps.

For large groups, it is recommended to remove a person from the circle for making a mistake or erroneously accusing someone. Soon, everyone will be laughing and cheering for the remaining ones.

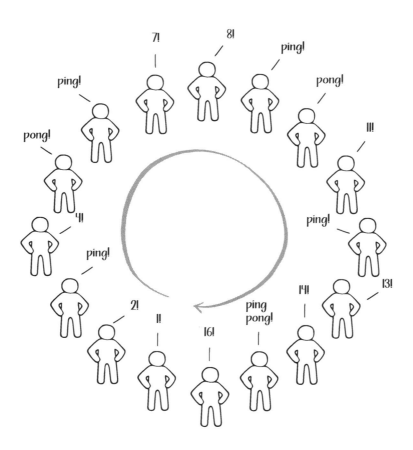

 **REMOTE-TEAM ADVICE**: This activity works well for remote teams. Use the communication tool of your preference. After a person says the number, ping or pong, they should also say the name of the next participant.

PEER INTRODUCTION GAME 📶

Peer Introduction Game is an activity for new team members to learn more about each other. A quick conversation followed by a peer introduction provides a quick mechanism to introduce each and every person on the large group.

RUNNING THE ACTIVITY:

1. Split the large group into pairs. Ask people to pair up with someone they don't know very well.

2. Ask the pairs to have a quick conversation about each other, and inform them that later they will introduce their pair. You can leave the conversation open or choose a few questions to be answered (such as: name, birth place, current role, favorite food, favorite travel location).

3. Go around the large group, and let everyone introduce their pair. *"Please meet Amit. He was born in Canada, but his family is from India. He enjoys Brazilian samba and his favorite food is hot-dog, especially when watching live baseball. He currently works as…"*

We have seen this activity being used on several different places and occasions. It works really well to have people say good things about each other, after having a quick one on one.

REMOTE-TEAM ADVICE: This activity works well for remote teams. Use the team's remote communication tool to pair up participants in separate chat rooms, then bring everybody to the same meeting/room and each person introduces their pair.

CARDINAL DIRECTIONS 📶

The Cardinal Directions activity is great for getting people moving, sharing things about each individual, while, at the same time, helping everyone understand the differences and similarities within a large group of people.

PREPARING FOR THE ACTIVITY:

* Set up a large room with space for everyone to move around.
* Draw a simple compass in the middle of the room (use tape and sticky note), marking North, South, East, and West directions.
* Identify the primary cardinals in the room walls. For instance: North—the window side, South—the door side, East—the projector side, and West—the nice painting side. It is more important to match a cardinal direction to a room wall than to be precise about the cardinal direction.
* Prepare a print-out page with interesting questions (yes/no style). There are some sample questions below. Feel free to create your own questions or ask people to create theirs during the activity.

RUNNING THE ACTIVITY:

1. Read one question, point to the North and tell it represents the yes answer. Then ask participants to move accordingly. Since the questions are a yes or no option, each person must select a side of the room, either yes or no, representing North or South.

2. Read another question, point to the East and tell it represents the yes answer. Then ask participants to move accordingly. Please note that they will now stand in one of the following four cardinals: N, W, E, or S.

3. Repeat it as long as you wish. Keep reading questions and asking people to move accordingly. Make sure to alternate between N-S and E-W movements. Please note that in any moment in time people will be standing in one of the four room corners.

This activity is very energizing and visual. It keeps everyone moving while being visual about the number of people representing each yes and no. At times, we would rather pass the print-out of questions around, asking people to either read one question or make a yes/no question. This gives everyone the opportunity to be creative with questions and perhaps find out specific information in which they are interested.

Sample yes/no questions:

* *On a Friday night, do you prefer staying at home rather than going out with friends?*
* *When keeping an appointment would you generally arrive at the last moment?*
* *Are you usually easy-going?*
* *In general, do you usually think carefully before speaking?*
* *At home, do you get irritated easily when things are not in their proper place?*
* *Do you often use your hands when talking?*
* *Do you find it easy to keep your emotions under control?*

* Do you find it difficult to go up to strangers at a social gathering and introduce yourself?
* Do other people normally know what you are doing or feeling without you telling them?
* Do you plan your activities well ahead of time?
* Do you usually complain when someone keeps you waiting?
* When you feel downhearted, do you normally find someone to cheer you up?
* Would you generally prefer to see a documentary rather than a comedy on TV?
* When you have made a big mistake at work, do you normally forget about it easily?
* When you see a picture hanging crooked on the wall, do you feel the urge to straighten it?
* Do you usually have specific goals and a definite sense of direction in your life?
* If someone in a social group expresses a point of view that differs from yours, would you normally keep quiet?
* Are you usually talkative when you are with people that you know?
* If you were renting a place, would you insist on a written agreement before paying your money?
* Do you often say or do things without thinking?
* When you have done something wrong, can you normally forget about it quickly and focus on the future?
* Do you sometimes keep quiet, fearing that people might criticize or laugh at you?

* *Do you often tell jokes and funny stories to your friends?*
* *Does your future on the whole seem promising and right to you?*
* *Do you frequently think about your future and the course your life is taking right now?*
* *After completing an important task do you often feel like you should have done it better?*

When closing the activity, you could say a message to raise the team building moment:

* *Some times we are close to someone, other times we are close to someone else.*
* *It varies at times, but it is essential to remember, we are all one team!*

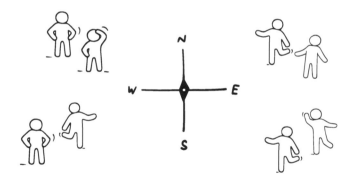

REMOTE-TEAM ADVICE: This activity works well for remote teams. Add the questions to an online polling tool and run it in real time with the team. After each round of questions, take a moment to acknowledge the answers and proceed.

FORMING TRIANGLES

Forming Triangles is a great energizer with a valuable message, being very useful for starting a conversation about self-organizing teams.

This activity is divided into two parts.

First part:

1. Ask the members of the group to walk individually in a random direction.
2. After some time, say the magic word "triangle": each group member will have to find two other people and form an equilateral triangle (each person is a triangle vertex and should point each arm towards the other two people representing the other triangle vertices; each person is a triangle vertex on one triangle only).
3. Track how long it took the group to form the triangles.

Second part:

1. Select one person to be the organizer of all triangles.
2. Ask the members of the group to walk in a random direction.
3. After some time, say the magic word "triangle": the organizer has to form equilateral triangles with all group members (including the organizer in one of the triangles).
4. Track how long it took the group to form the triangles.

The first part shows a self-organizing group; the second run shows a group guided by an organizer.

Typically, the self-organizing triangle formation runs faster than its counterpart, and the team feels more engaged in the activity. This activity fosters the conversation about an essential concept of successful agile teams: self-organization.

ZIP-ZAP-ZOOM 📶

Zip-Zap-Zoom is a good meeting starter, especially for new teams. It brings energy to the room and the activity dynamics helps participants remember each other's names.

RUNNING THE ACTIVITY:

1. Ask the team to form a circle, and each participant to close their hands while pointing index fingers.
2. Explain the rules to participants:

   Each participant should, in their turn, give a verbal command and point to a receiver. The verbal command should be one of the following:

   * **Zip:** Point to the person exactly at your side, keeping the previous direction.
   * **Zap:** Point to the person exactly at your side, changing the previous direction.
   * **Zoom:** Point to anyone in the circle, saying their name. The receiver should decide the direction for the next movement in their turn.

3. Ask a participant to make the first movement, giving one of the verbal commands and choosing the initial direction (clockwise or counterclockwise).

This activity not only is a good energizer but also pushes participants to focus, and helps them remember each other's names. For extra fun, have some markers for when a participant executes a wrong command and get them to buy snacks afterwards.

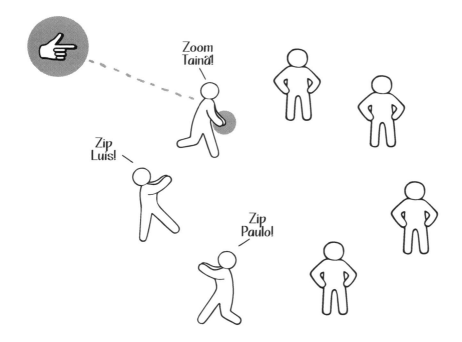

 **REMOTE-TEAM ADVICE**: This activity works well for remote teams. Share a remote board with the participants, then ask everyone to enter their name. Organize the names in a sequence and follow it for the activity.

BALLOON BATTLE

The Balloon Battle is a great energizer to get everyone moving while creating a situation to introduce some concepts like team strategy, team work, collaboration, partnership and win-win situations.

RUNNING THE ACTIVITY:

1. Instruct everyone to tie a balloon to their left foot (you will need balloons and strings for all participants).
2. Divide the large group into several smaller groups (for example, groups of three or four people).
3. Instruct everyone about the team's mission and the game's duration: *"All teams have the same goal: to protect the team balloons. The game lasts one minute. At the end we will count and announce the team with the highest number of full balloons."*
4. Say GO! and count down.

Typically, participants will have lots of fun. Many people might run around and attack other people's balloons.

At the end of the game you can have conversations about teamwork, team strategy, perception of responsibility, and our favorite: the competitive human nature, which at times works against a win-win situation.

For instance, if no one moves and attacks other people's balloons, every team accomplishes the goal of protecting the team's balloons and ends up with the highest number of full balloons. Interesting enough, we have never seen or heard about this outcome.

UNTANGLE YOURSELVES

Untangle Yourselves is a great energizer to get people moving. It has a very interesting message on finding your way out of a tangled situation.

RUNNING THE ACTIVITY:

1. Ask the group to form a circle.
2. Get everyone to put their hands up.
3. Give the tangling instructions.
   * With your right hand, grab someone's left hand.
   * With your left hand, grab someone's right hand.
   * You cannot grab the hands of people next to you.
4. Ask the group to untangle themselves without letting the hands go, and trying to form a circle.

Group size: larger than six people, up to any number. For very large groups, break into smaller groups of approximately 12 people.

The group will jump hands, switch around, and find a way out, forming either one or more circles. Sometimes, it is not possible to untangle. In such scenarios, ask the group to select one person to be removed. Hands that become free should reconnect to the person remaining in the tangled group.

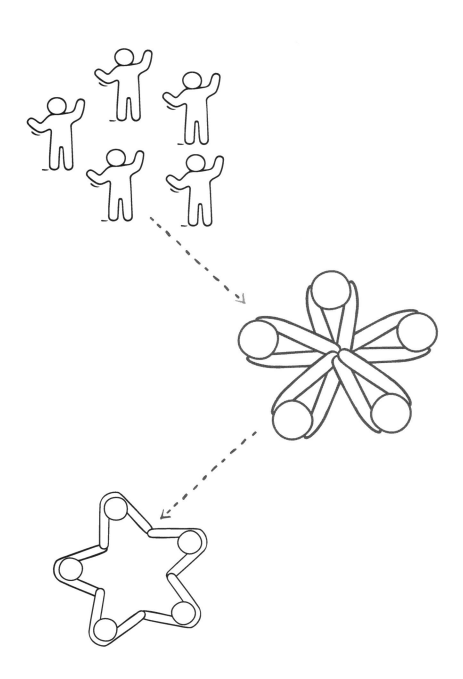

COMPLEX PIECES

Complex Pieces is a great energizer to get people moving around while fostering a conversation about complex systems and interconnected pieces.

RUNNING THE ACTIVITY:

1. Everybody stands up and walks around.
2. Each person thinks about two other people.
3. Without saying names, each person should stay equally distant from the two people they thought about. This should take one minute as people move around.
4. After people stop moving, ask the taller person in the group to move to a corner of the room.
5. Ask everyone to find their equal distances again.

This activity gets everyone energized while giving an opportunity to have a quick conversation about complex systems, changes and interconnected requirements. It works better for a group of ten to thirty people.

BACK TO BACK

Back to Back is a fun energetic activity with a strong and simple message about collaborative work, and the importance of aligning forces towards the same direction.

RUNNING THE ACTIVITY:

1. Instruct participants to find a pair of similar height and weight.
2. Ask everyone to sit on the floor, back to back with their pair.
3. Ask the pairs to hold their arms while keeping their backs together.
4. Tell everyone their goal is to stand up, while keeping arms and backs together.

This activity is really fun. People will laugh. Typically, a few pairs will be able to stand up faster, while others will have a hard time. Be sensitive to the group and only run this activity if appropriate.

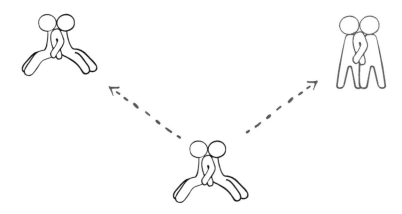

FIND YOUR PEERS

Find Your Peers is a really funny energizer to get everyone moving and laughing. It can be used for forming groups.

RUNNING THE ACTIVITY:

1. Decide how many groups you want to form at the end of the activity.
2. Choose one animal to represent each group.
3. Tell each participant which animal they represent, anonymously.
4. Ask everyone to move around in the room.
5. Instruct everyone to cover their eyes with their hands, make the animal noise, and try to find their group.

On step 3, instead of telling each person, you can write animal names in sticky notes and distribute them randomly.

We recommend being cautious about cultural differences and making sure participants are already used to energizers when you consider this activity.

COLLABORATIVE FACE DRAWING

Collaborative Face Drawing is a fun interactive activity that helps with name memorization.

RUNNING THE ACTIVITY:

1. Give each participant one index card and a pen.
2. Instruct participants to write their name on the bottom of the paper.
3. Ask everyone to walk randomly through the room until you say the word "stop."
4. Each person should pair up with someone nearby.
5. Instruct the pair to exchange papers.
6. Everyone should draw the other person's eyes.
7. Instruct the pairs to exchange papers again (now each person should have the paper with their name again).
8. Repeat steps 3 to 7 for all face parts (eyes, nose, ears, chin, hair, facial hair, and accessories).

Below are two moments from this activity. The first one shows step 3 in which everyone is walking randomly waiting for the stop command. The second image shows the final result: a collaborative face drawing.

This activity works well with different team sizes, it fosters quick one on one interactions between multiple people and the final artifacts are a fun memory from the meeting. You can display the drawings at the team area, for instance, or snap a photo for the future.

HUMAN ROCK-PAPER-SCISSORS 📶

Human Rock-Paper-Scissors is a fun, quick energizer activity that can be used to get everyone moving and laughing. Many people are familiar with the classic hand game, rock-paper-scissors. This is a variation of the game, but requires people to get on their feet, move, and act as a team, rather than an individual.

RUNNING THE ACTIVITY:

1. As a group, decide on a full-body pose that will signify each element (e.g. Rock — each person of one group will bend down and hug their knees and curl into a ball so they look like a rock; Scissors — each person of one group will stand with legs shoulder-width apart and both arms up and hands behind the head so they look like a scissor).

2. After the poses are decided, break participants into two groups. For each round, each group will need to do one of the poses (everyone in each group will need to do the same pose). Each group will have 20 seconds to strategize.

3. Once all of the groups have their poses decided, ask the two groups to face each other and count down from 3 (i.e. 3... 2... 1... SHOOT). On "SHOOT", each group will need to strike one of the three poses. Rock beats scissors, scissors beat paper, and paper beats rock.

4. Best out of five rounds wins.

This activity is especially fun because it can be modified to many different themes and variations. Have you heard about the great Canadian variation: Cowboy, Bear, and Ninja? Ninja kills the cowboy; cowboy kills the bear; bear kills the ninja.

ROCK   PAPER   SCISSORS

 REMOTE-TEAM ADVICE: This activity works well for remote teams. Share with the participants a remote board with three columns (rock, paper, scissors). Select the participants for each round. Instruct them to add their play (for instance, a sticky note with their name) under the respective column and submit it after a countdown ("3, 2, 1, SHOOT!"). You can do a tournament (three participants at a time) where the winners go to the semi-finals or finals (depending on the team size).

CHECK-IN

C heck-in activities gather information such as how participants feel towards the meeting and it is a good step to narrow down the themes that will be discussed in the meeting.

SAFETY CHECK 📶

The **Safety Check** is a fast and effective way to verify how safe people feel participating in the retrospective. It collects anonymous notes so that participants don't feel singled out or are intimidated to express themselves.

RUNNING THE ACTIVITY:

1. Ask participants to choose a number between 1 and 5 that indicates how safe they feel within the group and write it in a sticky note (the numbers should be taken anonymously, so everyone should use the same sticky note and pen color). Below you can see the meaning for each number:
   * **5:** No problem, I'll talk about anything.
   * **4:** I'll talk about almost anything; a few things might be hard.
   * **3:** I'll talk about some things, but others will be hard to say.
   * **2:** I'm not going to say much; I'll let others bring up issues.
   * **1:** I'm not going to talk at all, I don't feel safe.

2. Collect the sticky note from each participant (use a hat or some container to keep the activity anonymous).
3. Make the safety check result visible to the whole group.
4. Acknowledge the results and decide what's next.

WHAT TO DO WITH THE RESULTS?

Here is what can be said when:

- → **The safety is high:** "It seems like many folks in the room are up for talking about many topics, therefore it is worth moving to the next activity, which should trigger valuable conversations."
- → **The safety is medium:** "As we can see on the safety check results, some folks are not willing to talk about all topics. Let's keep this in mind and be respectful to each other's participation."
- → **The safety is low:** "As we can see on the safety check results, the group safety seems low. For this reason, let's use the remaining time and run an activity which might help us increase the group safety level."

Fostering a safe environment is a key element for any group activity. Acknowledging how the group feels allows you to act and address the situation. If the safety is low or medium, we recommend changing your main course activity to the Creating Safety activity.

Keep in mind that there are other activities that can be used as check-in, so change it up as needed.

 **REMOTE-TEAM ADVICE**: This activity works well for remote teams. Share a remote board with the participants, make sure that the notes will be completely anonymous, then ask everyone to enter their input.

ESVP: EXPLORER, SHOPPER, VACATIONER, PRISONER 📶

The **ESVP** is a short activity to measure participants' engagement for the meeting at hand.

1. Ask the participants to report anonymously their attitude toward the retrospective as an Explorer, Shopper, Vacationer or Prisoner.

   * **Explorers** — Are eager to discover new ideas and insights. They want to learn everything they can about the iteration/release/project.
   * **Shoppers** — Will look over all the available information and be happy to go home with one useful new idea.
   * **Vacationers** — Aren't interested in the work of the retrospective, but are happy to be away from the daily grind.
   * **Prisoners** — Feel they have been forced to attend and would rather be doing something else.

2. Collect the results and create a histogram to show the data.

3. Acknowledge the results and lead a discussion about what the results mean for the group.

This is a good variation for the Safety Check, as it asks about people participation from a different perspective. You can follow up with a variation of Creating Safety (" Why do you feel like a prisoner?").

This activity is described in the remarkable Agile Retrospectives book.[4]

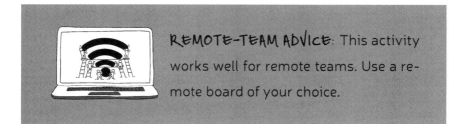

REMOTE-TEAM ADVICE: This activity works well for remote teams. Use a remote board of your choice.

---

[4] DERBY, Esther; LARSEN, Diana. *Agile Retrospectives: Making Good Teams Great.* Pragmatic Bookshelf, 2006.

HAPPINESS RADAR 📶

The **Happiness Radar** is very useful for opening a retrospective while narrowing down its context. It establishes a sequence for the retrospective, so participants first hear about people's feelings (on happiness) before going into a data gathering activity.

RUNNING THE ACTIVITY:

1. Decide and draw the target areas for collecting feedback on happiness (as table row titles). One suggestion is to have rows for people, technology, and processes.

"For the given context, I would like to know your feelings for each of these areas."

2. Draw the happy/ok/sad faces (as table column titles).

3. Ask the team to place their marks on the canvas:

"So, for each of the areas, please let us know how you felt on average. For instance, if you are always sad regarding technology, please make one mark on the technology/sad combination."

4. Optionally, decide upon sticky note color (for targeted areas) to use it as a color code for the activity that will come next.

Note that the target areas selected (row titles) should be very specific for the retrospective context and will influence the activities (and conversation) to follow.

It is really important to acknowledge how people feel, especially for a retrospective meeting. However, it is not easy for people to talk about emotions and it is even harder for them to connect emotions to the things that made them feel this way. The happiness radar provides a structure that helps with both.

We recommend you use the happiness radar activity with the same team periodically, keeping track of its results so you can compare how the team is feeling over time.

	☺	😐	☹
People	⊔	⊓	
Technology	|	∟	⊓
Process	☐	|	|

REMOTE-TEAM ADVICE: This activity works well for remote teams. Use a remote board of your choice.

HAPPINESS RADAR FOR A TIMELINE 🛜

Happiness Radar for a Timeline is a variation of the previous activity and gets the average happiness over a timeline. It works well for a release retrospective. The main difference for it and the typical happiness radar is that the column titles are time-based, instead of being area-specific.

RUNNING THE ACTIVITY:

1. Decide and draw the timeline for collecting feedback on happiness (as table column titles). One suggestion is to have milestones to remind the team of events that happened in that time (e.g., end of sprints, releases, someone joining the team).
   "Given the context, I would like to know your feelings during each of these points in time."
2. Draw the happy/ok/sad faces (as table row titles).
3. Ask the team to place their marks on the canvas:
   "So, for each of these moments, please let us know how you felt on average. For instance, if you were happy about our release 1, please make one mark on the release 1/happy cell."

This activity works well with large groups in which the context includes a long timeline for an event (for instance, from nine months ago since that event; last month; the past three days—from the day the event started until now).

	PROJECT BEGINS	RELEASE 1	RELEASE 2	TODAY
🙂	‖‖‖‖‖‖‖ ‖‖	‖ ‖‖‖‖‖ ‖ ‖	‖‖‖ ‖‖ ‖‖‖	‖‖‖‖‖‖‖‖ ‖‖‖‖‖‖‖
😐	‖ ‖ ‖	‖‖‖‖‖‖‖‖‖ ‖‖‖	‖‖‖‖‖ ‖	‖‖‖
🙁		‖ ‖‖	‖	‖‖

REMOTE-TEAM ADVICE: This activity works well for remote teams. Use a remote board of your choice.

ONE WORD 📶

The **One Word** is a simple check-in activity that allows participants to share their feelings before getting into the data and details for the meeting itself. It is a good opening for a meeting as it acknowledges people's feelings and gets them speaking from the very beginning.

RUNNING THE ACTIVITY:

1. Give each participant a pen and a sticky note.
2. Ask them to describe their feelings (for the meeting context) in one word.
3. Group the notes on an open canvas.
4. Optionally, ask if someone wants to share more about their selected word.

   "Please, describe how you feel in one word."

This activity is described as the check-in activity by Esther Derby and Diana Larsen in the remarkable *Agile Retrospectives* book.[5] It gets participants reflecting about the meeting's context, bringing everyone to the retrospective mindset. It also invites everyone to speak, which fosters further participation in the activities to follow.

---

[5] DERBY, Esther; LARSEN, Diana. *Agile Retrospectives: Making Good Teams Great*. Pragmatic Bookshelf, 2006.

ONE WORD

 **REMOTE-TEAM ADVICE**: This activity works well for remote teams. Use a remote board of your choice.

ANONYMOUS NOTE 📶

The **Anonymous Note** activity enables participants to signal this intention. At times, some participants want to bring up a point, but do not want to start the conversation about it.

RUNNING THE ACTIVITY:

1. Write down the following sentence on the board: Are you ok reading your note out loud?
2. Explain that you will ask them to write down a few notes on the following activity, and you want to check that everyone is comfortable reading out their notes.
3. Instruct participants to write a Y or N on a sticky note and fold it. Y for "yes," N for "no, I don't feel comfortable reading some of the notes I will bring up today."
4. Collect the notes anonymously and place them on the board.
5. Share the results with the group.

In case there is at least one N, you should not use an activity that requires participants to read their notes out loud. Otherwise, you are free to ask participants to read their notes before placing it on the board or even ask openly: who wrote this note?

We have participated in several retrospectives. It is really embarrassing when someone asks who wrote something and no one answers. This quick check-in activity helps avoid this situation.

ARE YOU OK READING ALL YOUR NOTES?

REMOTE-TEAM ADVICE: This activity works well for remote teams. Use a remote board of your choice.

DRAW YOUR FEELINGS 📶

Draw your feelings is a great check-in activity for helping people express feelings for a retrospective meeting. Drawing enables people to express their emotions. Thus, it is a good starter before the main course activity, where participants typically will write notes and verbalize things and actions for the given context.

RUNNING THE ACTIVITY:

1. Distribute sticky note notes and a sharpie for each participant.
2. Write the following sentence on the canvas: "How do you feel?"
3. Ask participants: "Please draw something that better expresses how you feel right now, in the context of this meeting" (consider saying vehicle, animal, object, super-hero or view instead of "something").
4. Ask participants to place their sticky note with the drawing on the common canvas, and, if they want, to say something about their drawing.

We have done this activity asking people to draw vehicles, animals, and objects. This activity is similar to the one word activity, but with drawings instead of words to express feelings.

The main idea behind "draw your feelings" is to express a specific emotion, feeling or situation that you can't normally express with words. Drawing it helps people later verbalize the reason behind it.

Therefore, it is a great check-in activity, for two reasons: (1) allow the individual to first express feelings via drawings, before writing about it, and (2) make it visible about how the group is feeling before entering the main activity.

REMOTE-TEAM ADVICE: This activity works well for remote teams. Ask participants to draw with pen and paper and share it in the communication tool.

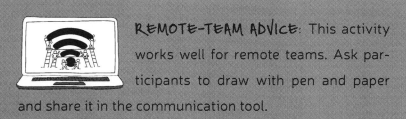

MAIN COURSE: TEAM BUILDING

A group of people does not turn into a team overnight. Team building activities help new teams emerge and work together.

DEFINING THE TEAM VISION STATEMENT 🛜

The **Defining Team Vision Statement** provides an overall statement summarizing, at the highest level, the unique position that the team intends to fill in the organization.

RUNNING THE ACTIVITY:

1. Write the team vision statement template on the whiteboard (or a common canvas):
   * For (target organization)
   * Who (statement of the need or opportunity)
   * The (team name, identity) is a (team classification, category)
   * That (team singularity, compelling reason for the team existence)
   * Unlike (current alternative without the team)
   * Our team (statement of primary differentiation)
2. Divide the team into smaller groups and ask each group to fill in a blank separately (or more than one, depending on the size of the team).
3. Gather the results of each group, forming a unique sentence.

While running this activity, the team vision statement template provides a short motivating set of words, summarizing and encapsulating the principle elements of the team's vision and identity. After being created, the team vision statement communicates the intent and the importance of the team to the overall organization and concerned people.

Below, there is a sample statement created from this activity:

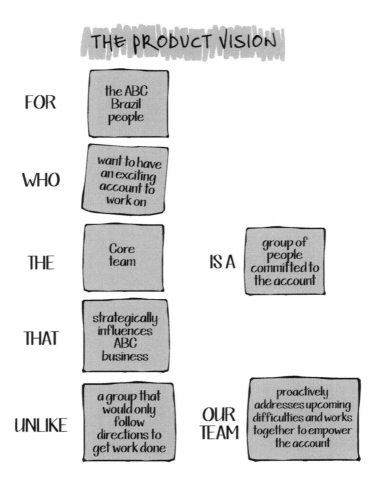

THE PRODUCT VISION

FOR — the ABC Brazil people

WHO — want to have an exciting account to work on

THE — Core team — IS A — group of people committed to the account

THAT — strategically influences ABC business

UNLIKE — a group that would only follow directions to get work done — OUR TEAM — proactively addresses upcoming difficulties and works together to empower the account

REMOTE-TEAM ADVICE: This activity works well for remote teams. Use a remote board of your choice.

THE TEAM IS – IS NOT – DOES – DOES NOT 📶

The Team Is - Is Not - Does - Does Not helps define a team. Sometimes, it's easier to describe something by saying what this thing is not or does not do. This activity seeks to explain this way, asking specifically each positive and negative aspect about the team and what it is or what it does.

RUNNING THE ACTIVITY:

1. Divide a white canvas in four areas (Is / Is Not / Does / Does Not).
2. Write the name of the team above the quadrants.
3. Ask each participant to describe the team on sticky notes and put them on the correspondent areas.
4. Read and group the similar notes.
   * The team is...
   * The team is not...
   * The team does...
   * The team does not...

This activity helps explain the team. Typically, after this activity participants will have a more consensual view of what the team does as well as what the team doesn't do. The discussions that happen during this activity help the team to clarify strategic decisions, such as "this is something the team will never do" or "but this other one is our responsibility".

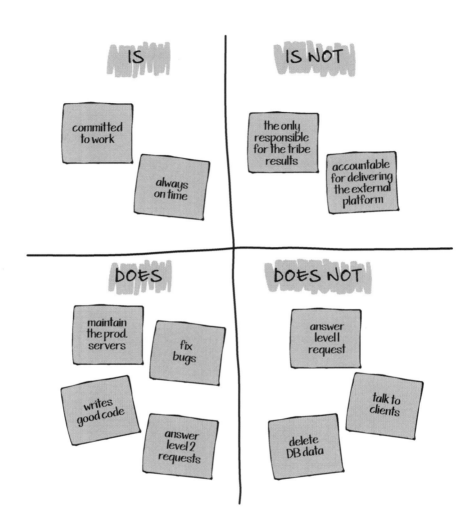

IS

committed to work

always on time

IS NOT

the only responsible for the tribe results

accountable for delivering the external platform

DOES

maintain the prod. servers

fix bugs

writes good code

answer level 2 requests

DOES NOT

answer level 1 request

talk to clients

delete DB data

REMOTE-TEAM ADVICE: This activity works well for remote teams. Use a remote board of your choice.

UNDERSTANDING THE GROUP KNOWLEDGE 📶

Understanding the Group Knowledge is a team building activity that helps the team understand the group knowledge and abilities, as well as the intentions and actions towards increasing it.

RUNNING THE ACTIVITY:

1. Ask all the participants to list all knowledge and abilities we believe a team like ours should have.

2. For each item, answer the following question: How do you feel as a group about these? Please place the listed items at the appropriate area:

   * **We know that we know** – it is clear to the whole group that we do have this knowledge.

   * **We didn't know that we knew** – the knowledge existed within the group, but it was not clear to the whole group that we had this knowledge.

   * **We didn't know that we didn't know** – the knowledge does not exist within the group and no one was aware of it.

   * **We know that we don't know** – the knowledge does not exist within the group, but we were aware of it.

3. Give participants another chance to list items to the "we didn't know that we don't know" quadrant:

   "So think again about the things we didn't know. Things of which we weren't aware. Things we have to investigate fur-

*ther in order to understand and figure out what it is that we
don't know."*

4. Have a conversation about the items on "we know that we know",
as well as the desire to move all important knowledge to this
quadrant.

5. Read the items for the three remaining quadrants and mark the intent to move such items according to the following questions (consider drawing arrows for indicating the items' movement):

   * What are the items we should move from "we didn't know that
   we knew" to "we know that we know"?

   * What are the items we should move from "we didn't know that
   we didn't know" to "we know that we don't know"?

   * What are the items we should move from "we know that we
   don't know" to "we know that we know"?

6. Add action items on a different post it color to indicate the actions
individuals are doing for improving the team's knowledge.

Ignorance is not a bliss! Despite the popular saying, an effective group of people must understand the overall group knowledge.
This activity is very useful in clarifying that and, even more important, it enables the team to align the actions they want to take
towards increasing the group's knowledge. This activity is inspired
by the conscious competence learning model, also known as the
four stages of competence.[6]

---

[6]   CURTISS, Paul; WARREN, Phillip. *The Dynamics of Life Skills Coaching*. Prince Albert, 1974.

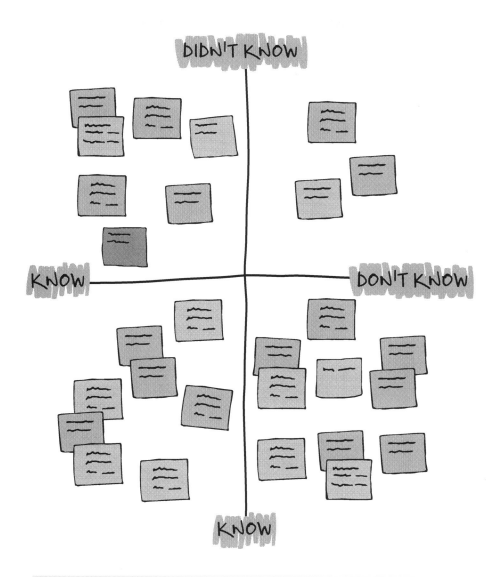

REMOTE-TEAM ADVICE: This activity works well for remote teams. Use a remote board of your choice.

CREATING SAFETY 📶

Creating Safety allows participants to bring up whatever was making them uncomfortable on the safety check. A low safety compromises any meeting, so don't hold on to your agenda if that happens—instead, work on creating safety.

RUNNING THE ACTIVITY:

1. Ask for insights on what could be bringing the safety level down:

   "So, put yourself in the shoes of someone who is not feeling safe to talk about some topics. What could be the causes? Please write these on a yellow sticky note and place it on the board."

   This sentence is quite powerful. The safety check is anonymous, but this opens the door for things to be raised in a subtle way. One does not need to say, "I feel unsafe in this or that." Instead, issues are raised without a first person. This should unearth the causes of lower safety.

2. Group the causes on the board based on similarity.

3. Ask participants for ideas on how to make people feel safe given the causes:

   "Think about the things you could do to help overcome these causes on the board (on one color of sticky notes); please write them on an another color of sticky note and place it next to the cause."

4. Read out all the notes and have a (careful) guided conversation on these. Use your judgement on how to read the notes and conduct

the conversation. You should keep in mind that some people might be uncomfortable with some topics and ideas, so do not jump into any conclusions or get people into the spotlight.

5. Run the safety check again.

Hopefully, the safety will go up. The important thing is that the safety check results were taken into account and participants (safely) talked about it.

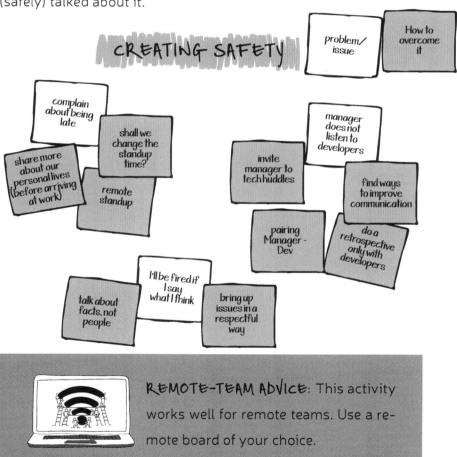

REMOTE-TEAM ADVICE: This activity works well for remote teams. Use a remote board of your choice.

360 DEGREES APPRECIATION 📶

The **360 Degrees Appreciation** is a team-building activity to foster open appreciation feedback within a team. It is especially useful to increase team morale and improve personal relationships.

RUNNING THE ACTIVITY:

1. Give paper and pen to each participant.
2. Ask everyone to write down what they appreciate on all the other participants (recommended time: two minutes per participant).
3. Ask the group to form a circle.
4. Ask one participant to sit in the center of this circle.
5. Everyone in the circle should read the appreciation feedback to the participant in the center (complete the 360 degrees).
6. Change the participant in the center until everyone has received feedback.

Typically, the 360 Degrees Appreciation activity inspires constant feedback, strengthening relationships and trust. Often, the responses and results are quite enthusiastic and the team moral gets a boost. This activity is based on the 360 degree feedback practice.

360 DEGREES APPRECIATION

REMOTE-TEAM ADVICE: This activity works well for remote teams. Share a remote board with the participants, then ask everyone to enter their name. Organize the names in a sequence and follow it for the activity, each time with a different participant receiving the feedback.

GENERAL BEHAVIOR ACTIVITY 📶

The **General Behavior Activity** fosters a team conversation about behavior. It is especially useful when forming new teams. The results of this activity serve as an ongoing guide for acceptable and unacceptable team behavior.

RUNNING THE ACTIVITY:

1. Separate the canvas in two areas with the following titles:
   * Wonderful behavior.
   * Unacceptable behavior.
2. Ask participants to write down examples of wonderful behavior and unacceptable behavior on sticky notes and place them on the canvas.
3. Discuss about the notes with the group.

Talking about behavior is important at any time, and it is especially important while forming a team. More than that, it is much easier to talk about desirable and undesirable behaviors that haven't happened, helping set the expectation for the future.

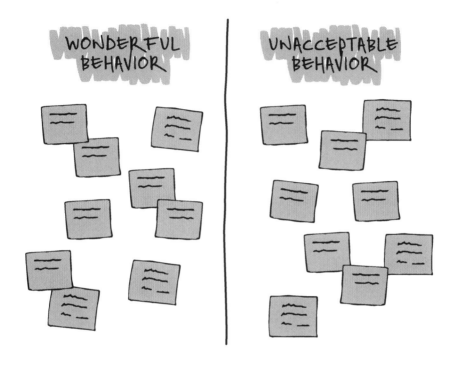

REMOTE-TEAM ADVICE: This activity works well for remote teams. Use a remote board of your choice.

THAT PERSON & THIS PERSON 📶

That Person & This Person is a team-building activity that fosters a conversation on being a team player. The results of this activity serve as an ongoing guide for acceptable and unacceptable team behavior.

RUNNING THE ACTIVITY:

1. Separate the canvas in two separate areas with the following sentences (drawing is very welcome):
   * Don't be "that person."
   * "This person rocks!

2. Ask participants to write comments on sticky notes and put them under this and that person.

   "'That person' is a non-team player. 'This person' is the ultimate team player. Everyone wants 'this person' on their team! Please go back in time and think about everyone with whom you have ever worked. Without mentioning names, please write down (on separate sticky notes) what you liked the most and the least about this and that person."

3. Discuss about the notes in the group. Consider grouping them together.

Talking about behavior can be difficult. Framing it this way ("that person did this, this person did that") makes it easier for participants to express their feelings about behaviors with examples.

REMOTE-TEAM ADVICE: This activity works well for remote teams. Use a remote board of your choice.

TRADE-OFF SLIDERS 📶

Trade-off Sliders is a team-building activity for creating and documenting a common understanding for trade-offs. Many decisions and conversations are based on individual views and assumptions between choices. A few examples: What is most valuable, quality of work or delivery speed? Compliance to the process or efficiency? Making more money or spending more time with family? Company finance or employee happiness?

RUNNING THE ACTIVITY:

1. Explain to the team what trade-offs are:

   "Trade-off is an exchange in which you give up one thing in order to get something else you also desire. Effective teamwork is directly related to team members' ability to make decisions based on the team's (common) understanding of trade-offs."

2. Write down the categories under comparison on sticky notes. Write them as a group activity. Try to eliminate duplicates.

3. Place the categories on the canvas as row titles, then draw a horizontal line for each category.

4. Draw vertical lines (same number as horizontal lines). Write highest on top of the left-most line and lowest on top of the right-most line.

5. Ask participants to mark their initials on several sticky notes and place one per row. The constraint: each column must have

one sticky note with their initials (e.g. only one of the categories will be marked on the highest column line).

6. Trade-offs equalization: with a different sticky note color, decide as a group how each category relates to the other. The steps above make this conversation easier as group agreements and disagreements are very visible on the canvas.

This activity fosters an open conversation based on a visible and collaborative canvas. Making trade-offs very clear will avoid future disagreements and will fasten decisions.

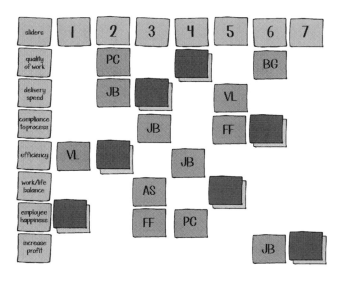

REMOTE-TEAM ADVICE: This activity works well for remote teams. Use a remote board of your choice.

ROLE EXPECTATIONS MATRIX 📶

Role Expectations Matrix is a team-building activity that aims to map out the expectations among team members. It helps them better define their roles and avoid future conflicts due to hidden or unknown expectations.

RUNNING THE ACTIVITY:

1. Create a list of all the team members' roles.

2. Using the list, create a matrix with the list of roles along both horizontal and vertical axes. Label the vertical axis as "from" and the horizontal axis as "to."

3. Ask team members to write down (on separate sticky notes) their expectations to each one of the roles. These notes should go on the cells on a horizontal line for the team member role.

4. Discuss among the group the whole matrix. We recommend selecting one "from" role (a matrix vertical line) and then each person reads their expectation notes for that role. Repeat for all roles.

The goal in completing the matrix is to find the most complete picture of team members' expectations on each other. This activity is inspired on the give-and-take matrix from the *Gamestorming* book.[7]

---

[7]   GRAY, Dave; BROWN, Sunni; MACANUFO, James. *Gamestorming: A Playbook For Innovators, Rulebreakers, And Changemakers.* O'Reilly Media, 2010.

ROLE EXPECTATION MATRIX

FROM \ TO	DEV	QA	PM	PO
DEV				
QA				
PM				
PO				

REMOTE-TEAM ADVICE: This activity works well for remote teams. Use a remote board of your choice.

DELEGATION MAP 🛜

The **Delegation Map** activity helps clarify the expectation and delegation level between two individuals or two groups (A and B). It is a team-building activity that lists and defines the delegation level for each specific aspect for their work agreement.

RUNNING THE ACTIVITY:

1. Introduce the concept of delegation to the team: "Delegation is the assignment of responsibility or authority to another person to carry out specific activities."

2. Identify A and B, the "delegator" and the "delegated" (e.g. A — manager, B — team; A — father, B — son; A — Infra team, B — Development team).

3. Write down the key areas to be considered on sticky notes. Write them as a group activity. Try eliminating duplicates.

4. Place the key areas on the canvas as column titles, then draw a vertical line for each area.

5. Write the following delegation levels as row titles:
   * **Tell** — A makes a decision and communicates it to B.
   * **Sell** — A makes a decision and convinces B it is right.
   * **Consult** — A has a decision ready, but shapes it based on B's input.
   * **Join** — Decisions are made with equal authority between A and B.

* **Advise** – B prepares a decision with input from A before finalizing it.
* **Confirm** – B makes a decision and seeks buy-in from A;
* **Delegate** – A passes off a decision to B without influencing it.

6. Draw horizontal lines for each delegation level, forming a map for all key areas and the seven delegation levels.

7. As a group, define the delegation level for each area, marking it with a sticky note.

Delegation is much more than a "yes" or "no" question, it is about setting expectations. The results from this activity are a concrete, visible artifact that the team can refer to in the future.

This activity is based on the seven levels of authority[8] as defined by Jurgen Appelo, author of *Management 3.0*.[9]

---

[8] APPELO, Jurgen. *Leading Agile Developers: The Seven Levels of Authority*. Available at: <InformIT.com>. Access on: December, 2013.

[9] APPELO, Jurgen. *Management 3.0: Leading Agile Developers, Developing Agile Leaders*. Addison-Wesley Professional, 2011.

DELEGATION MAP

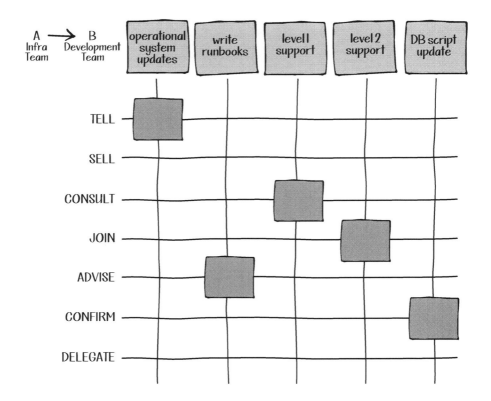

A → B
Infra Team   Development Team

Columns: operational system updates | write runbooks | level 1 support | level 2 support | DB script update

Rows: TELL | SELL | CONSULT | JOIN | ADVISE | CONFIRM | DELEGATE

REMOTE-TEAM ADVICE: This activity works well for remote teams. Use a remote board of your choice.

GROUND RULES 🛜

Ground Rules help with team formation. The activity is especially useful for collectively deciding and writing down the team ground rules. Discussing ground rules after problems arise is much more difficult.

RUNNING THE ACTIVITY:

1. Create the empty canvas with the ground rules elements:
   * **Process:** How the activities will be carried out;.
   * **Norms:** Ways in which team members will interact with each other.
2. Ask participants to write down the rules they feel really strongly about (e.g. Norm – everyone should keep Skype open while in the office).
3. Discuss among the group and decide about each rule.

It is quite common to define ground rules before playing a game. When rules are defined or changed after the game starts, people get uncomfortable and may consider it unfair. Likewise, define team norms and processes while the team is still being formed.

In some situations, you might see yourself in the middle of a game and rules are not clear at all. Stop and define the ground rules.

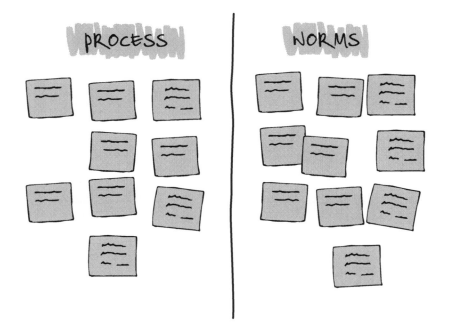

REMOTE-TEAM ADVICE: This activity works well for remote teams. Use a remote board of your choice.

DEFINING THE TEAM PRINCIPLES 📶

The **Defining the Team Principles** activity helps the team collectively define and write down the team principles they want to follow. It fosters an upfront and democratic conversation about team principles.

RUNNING THE ACTIVITY:

1. Introduce the activity, adding more discussion areas as necessary:

   "Let's have a conversation on how we will deal with one another on an ongoing basis. Collectively, we will write down the team principles for each of these areas."

   * Meetings structure and schedule.
   * Preferred method of communication.
   * Roles and availability.
   * Process.

2. Split the canvas into the number of identified areas (in this example: Meetings – Communication – Roles – Process).

3. Ask for individual notes.

   "Please write down your notes on team principles for each of the identified areas. You should use the sticky note color accordingly."

   * Constraints (on a sticky note of one color).
   * Strong recommendation (on a sticky note of a different color).

4. Discuss among the group and take notes (consider writing action items on sticky notes with another color).

Define the team principles while the team is still being formed. It will help the team be more efficient, by having agreed upon principles to refer to.

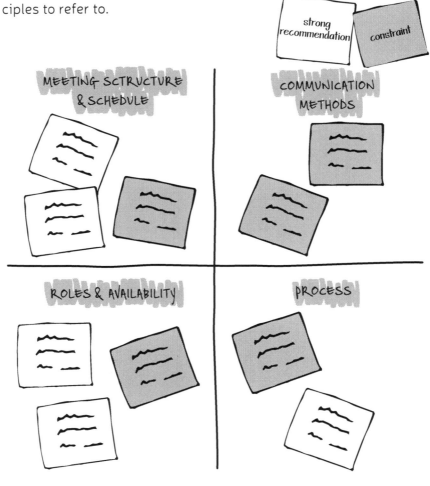

REMOTE-TEAM ADVICE: This activity works well for remote teams. Use a remote board of your choice.

CANDY LOVE

Candy Love is a great team-building activity that gets participants talking about their life beyond the work activities.

RUNNING THE ACTIVITY:

1. Place a package of M&M's, Skittles or another colorful candy in a jar.
2. Ask a participant to pick up a candy from the jar, and then share something personal according to the candy color:
   * **Red:** One thing that you love about your job. This candy will inspire people to see the positive side about their work.
   * **Yellow:** A life goal you are working on. This gives everyone positive vibes and inspiration.
   * **Green:** Your favorite book or movie. Everyone has hobbies and past-time recreations so it is definitely a great candy to divert their attention to the things they love to do.
   * **Purple:** Favorite way to revive yourself during the workday. This kind of de-stresses their minds thinking about spa, movie, bonding with the family, etc.
   * **Blue:** One stressful thing about your job you wish you could improve. This one is actually motivating, since it will convert every negative thing about their job into something positive.
   * **Orange:** Your favorite food. Everyone loves food. It is a topic that really picks up everyone's interest.

3. Pass the jar to the next participant and go back to step 2.

4. Stop when the candies or the time is over.

This activity is especially useful for the early stages of a team formation, as it helps people open up and talk about hobbies, food, and other very important aspects of their life.

ROLES WE PLAY 📶

Roles We Play is a team-building activity to trigger a conversation about all the roles we play in our lives. It is especially useful for a diverse group of people that starts working together. Typically, the group' bonding will increase once they get to know the many roles each one plays aside their current job description.

RUNNING THE ACTIVITY:

1. Read Wayne Dyer's quote:

   "Your life is like a play with several acts. Some of the characters who enter have short roles to play, others, much larger. Some are villains and others are good guys. But all of them are necessary; otherwise, they wouldn't be in the play. Embrace them all, and move on to the next act."[10]

2. Draw the week schedule, including slots for before work, work hours, after work, and weekends and holidays.

3. Ask participants to write each role they play on a different sticky note (with their initials on it) and place them in the most appropriate slot on the week schedule.

4. Affinity grouping by common roles (e.g.: pet owner, dog owner, cat daddy).

5. Group conversation about all the roles played by all participants.

---

[10] DYER, Wayne. *Change your thoughts*. Available at: <https://www.drwaynedyer.com>. Access on: May, 2020.

Typically, many notes (sticky notes) will be placed on the week schedule and people will openly talk about many roles they play. A good way to close the meeting is by saying a few words such as:

"As we all can see on the board, there are many roles we play. I am sure you learned something new about each person in this room. For instance, next time you say good morning to Bob you can ask him about his early-morning yoga."

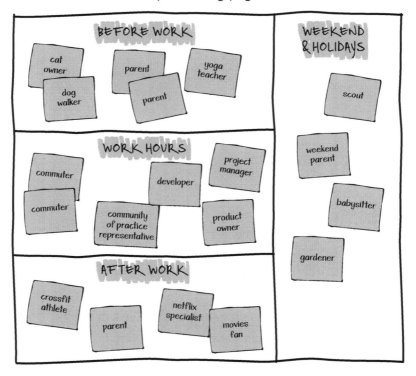

REMOTE-TEAM ADVICE: This activity works well for remote teams. Use a remote board of your choice.

SWOT – STRENGTHS, WEAKNESSES, OPPORTUNITIES, THREATS ⌁

SWOT is a team-building activity that helps team members better understand each other's strengths and weaknesses, as well as find opportunities and threats they might face together. It is a good activity for when a project is starting or when new members have joined an existing team.

RUNNING THE ACTIVITY

1. Draw the four quadrants: Strengths, Weaknesses, Opportunities, Threats.

2. Introduce the first two areas:
   * **Strengths:** write down what you feel you do well that can help the team.
   * **Weaknesses:** what are the things that you could improve?

3. Give the team time to write down notes for those areas.

4. Read all strengths and weaknesses out loud, clarifying if needed, but not fostering discussion yet.

5. Introduce the other two areas:
   * **Opportunities:** given the team's strengths, what can you capitalize on and take as a lead to be successful?
   * **Threats:** with those weaknesses, what are the obstacles you will have to overcome?

6. Give the team time to write notes for those two areas.

7. Group discussion.

We found this activity on Innovation Games.[11] It has been an effective exercise to get team members to know each other better and work as a group to improve. Often, team members will find opportunities in others' strengths, which they hadn't thought about before!

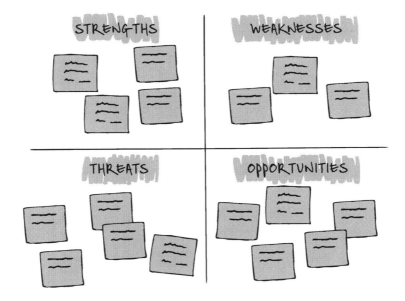

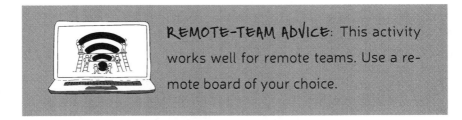

REMOTE-TEAM ADVICE: This activity works well for remote teams. Use a remote board of your choice.

---

[11] HOHMANN, Luke. *Innovation Games*. Available at: <https://www.innovationgames.com>. Access on: May, 2020.

MAIN COURSE: RETROSPECTIVES, LOOKING BACK

Teams that have retrospective as a recurring meeting will typically look for main course alternatives. By varying the activity, the team can look at different angles and perspectives, therefore generating new insights.

WELL, NOT SO WELL, NEW IDEAS 📶

Well, Not So Well, New Ideas is commonly used to bring conversations about the positive notes, the improvements and suggestions that the team has in mind.

RUNNING THE ACTIVITY:

1. Split the canvas into three areas:
    *   **Well** — things that went well, that moves us forward, helps us get better. We want to repeat these!
    *   **Not so well** — things that went wrong, that need improvement, that hold us back. We want to eliminate or avoid these!
    *   **New ideas** — things that we should consider trying, suggestions, new ideas.
2. Ask participants to add notes to each of the three areas.
3. Conversations and action items.

This is a very common retrospective activity. It is direct and straight to the point: What went well? Not so well? Do you have any new ideas? It is definitely a great option for teams getting used to retrospectives.

REMOTE-TEAM ADVICE: This activity works well for remote teams. Use a remote board of your choice.

PEAKS AND VALLEYS TIMELINE 🛜

Peaks and Valleys Timeline provides a simple visual language for sharing individual views on the ups and downs for a given timeline. It is an effective way for a large group to visualize and uncover events and their interconnections.

RUNNING THE ACTIVITY:

1. Draw a horizontal arrow representing the timeline on the bottom of the canvas. Define the start and the end of the timeline.

2. Decide upon the canvas vertical gradient. For instance, the happiness gradient, where the very top is the happiest and the very bottom is the saddest.

3. Invite a participant to draw their Peaks and Valleys timeline: *"Starting on the beginning of the timeline, and keeping the marker on the canvas the whole time. Please share your Peaks and Valleys timeline. You should do so by drawing the line and speaking at the same time."*

4. Invite more participants to draw their timeline (one at a time). Consider using a different marker color or line pattern.

At the end of this activity the whole group will have a view of several Peaks and Valleys Timelines. It is a good activity for getting participants to open up for further conversation. It is also very useful for correlating events with the chosen gradient (team feelings on the example below) and for recognizing contradiction —such as ups and downs for the same event.

The Peaks and Valleys Timeline activity is also known as Cliffs and Valleys or Emotional Seismograph.

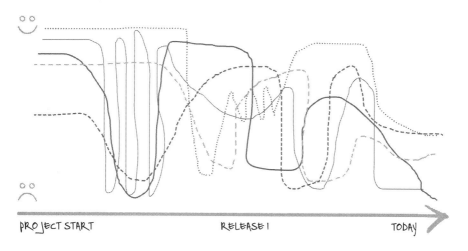

PEAKS & VALLEYS TIMELINE

PROJECT START   RELEASE 1   TODAY

REMOTE-TEAM ADVICE: This activity works well for remote teams. Use a remote board with free drawing of your choice.

EMPATHY SNAP ON BIG HITTER MOMENTS 📶

Empathy Snap on Big Hitter Moments is a great activity that gets participants guessing each other's big hitter moments.

RUNNING THE ACTIVITY:

1. Give each team member two index cards of different colors and a marker pen.
2. On the first card, hidden from the others, they should write their "big hitter" moment (a special moment in which they were involved).
3. On the second card they should write their name at the top and place it on the table.
4. Once all team members have handed in their name card, each team member takes a name card from the pile, ensuring they do not have their own.
5. On this card, they will write what they think is the big hitter for the person whose name is on the card, and keep the card. Essentially, they should try to guess what that person has written on their hidden card.
6. Once all the name cards have been completed with a big hitter, a team member reads out the name of the team member written on the card and their guess at the big hitter for that person.
7. The named person then reads out what their big hitter actually was.
8. If there is a match, then SNAP!
9. The exercise continues until all team members have read out their guesses and have responded with their actual big hitter.

This activity helps make people feel great. They have to think about something great they did and get to hear compliments by others. It is great for elevating team morale.

This activity was originally described by Matthew Skelton.[12] We changed it slightly, keeping the big hitter for cool things only, and also changed the activity period for whichever is identified by the group.

REMOTE-TEAM ADVICE: This activity works well for remote teams. Ask participants to take their notes with pen and paper. Decide and follow a sequence of participants. Then the group should guess each person's moment. Consider having a SNAP sound prepared to play when there is a match.

---

[12] SKELTON, Matthew. *Empathy Snap*. Available at: <http://blog.matthewskelton.net/2012/11/15/icebreaker-for-agile-retrospectives-empathy-snap/>. Access on: December, 2013.

REPEAT/AVOID 📶

Repeat/Avoid is a simple and effective data-gathering activity. It is based on two very specific questions: What to repeat? What to avoid?

RUNNING THE ACTIVITY:

1. Ask participants to add their notes accordingly:
   * What should we repeat?
   * What should be avoided?
2. Group the notes and discuss.

This is a common retrospective activity for data gathering. It is an alternative to keep the team engaged while slightly changing the format.

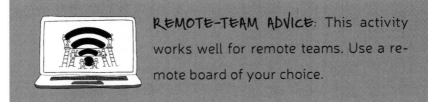

REMOTE-TEAM ADVICE: This activity works well for remote teams. Use a remote board of your choice.

SPEED CAR 📶

Speed Car is a simple activity for helping the team identify things that make them move faster, and things that slow them down.

RUNNING THE ACTIVITY:

1. Ask participants to write notes and place them on the following two areas: Engine and Parachute.
   * **Engine:** What has been pushing us forward? Making us move faster?
   * **Parachute:** What has been slowing us down?
2. Group the notes and discuss.

This is a common retrospective activity for data gathering. It is an alternative to keep the team engaged while slightly changing the format.

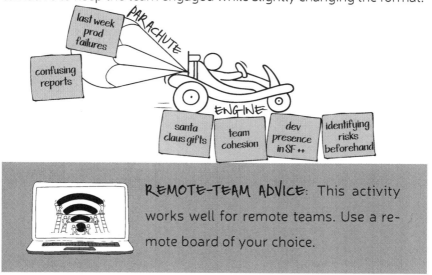

REMOTE-TEAM ADVICE: This activity works well for remote teams. Use a remote board of your choice.

HOT-AIR BALLOON 🛜

Hot-air Balloon is a simple activity for helping the team identify things that makes them move faster, and things that slow them down.

RUNNING THE ACTIVITY:

1. Ask participants to write notes and place them on the following two areas: Fire and hot air, and Forces pulling down.
   * **Fire and hot air:** What helps us go higher? What are the things that push us forward?
   * **Forces pulling down:** Which are the forces pulling us down?
2. Group the notes and discuss.

This is a common retrospective activity for data gathering. It is an alternative to keep the team engaged while slightly changing the format.

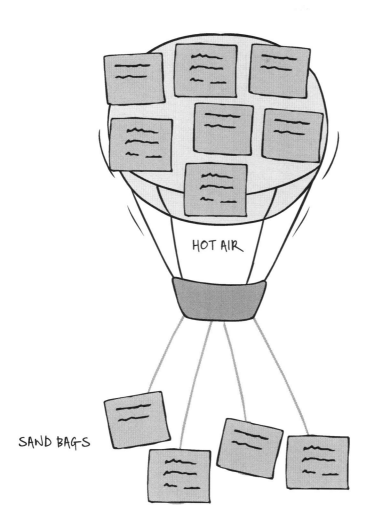

HOT AIR

SAND BAGS

REMOTE-TEAM ADVICE: This activity works well for remote teams. Use a remote board of your choice.

ANCHORS AND ENGINE 📶

Anchors and Engine is a simple activity for helping the team identify things that make them move faster and things that slow them down.

RUNNING THE ACTIVITY:

1. Ask participants to write notes and place them on the following two areas: Engine and Anchors.
   * **Engine:** What is the fuel for our engine? What are the things that push us forward?
   * **Anchors:** What is holding us back, or slowing us down?
2. Group the notes and discuss.

This is a common retrospective activity for data gathering. It is an alternative to keep the team engaged while slightly changing the format.

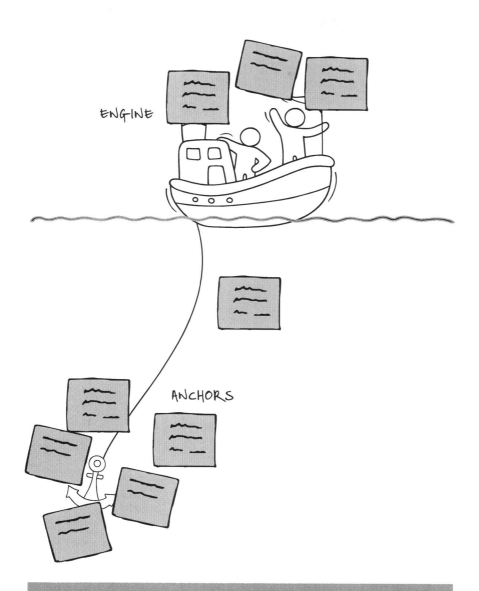

ENGINE

ANCHORS

REMOTE-TEAM ADVICE: This activity works well for remote teams. Use a remote board of your choice.

WWW: WORKED WELL, KINDA WORKED, DIDN'T WORK 📶

WWW is a great data gathering activity for retrospectives, guiding the discussion to team practices.

RUNNING THE ACTIVITY:

1. Split the canvas into three areas:
   1. **Worked well** – things that worked really well.
   2. **Kinda worked** – things that kind of worked, but you rather tweak them a little bit.
   3. **Didn't work** – things that did not work.
2. Ask participants for their notes.
3. Group the notes by affinity and discuss them.

This is a common retrospective activity for data gathering. It is an alternative to keep the team engaged while slightly changing the format.

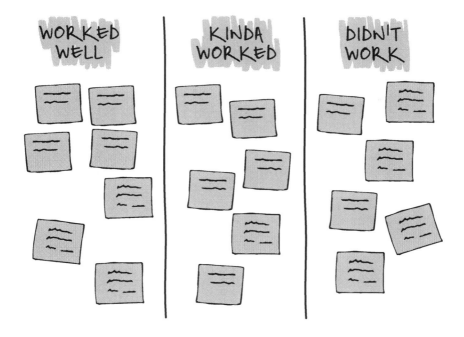

 **REMOTE-TEAM ADVICE:** This activity works well for remote teams. Use a remote board of your choice.

KALM - KEEP, ADD, MORE, LESS 🛜

KALM is a retrospective activity that fosters the conversation about current activities and their perceived value. It helps team members understand each other's perceived value off such practices.

RUNNING THE ACTIVITY:

1. Split the canvas into four areas:
   * **Keep** — something the team is doing well and whose value you recognize the value.
   * **Less** — something already being done, but of which you rather do less.
   * **More** — something already being done which believe will bring more value if done even more.
   * **Add** — a new idea or something you have seen working before that you would like to bring to the table.
2. Ask participants for their notes.
3. Group the notes by affinity and discuss.

This is a common retrospective activity for data gathering. It is an alternative to keep the team engaged while slightly changing the format.

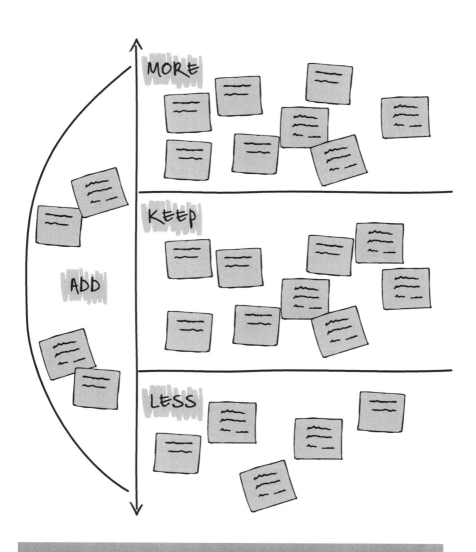

 REMOTE-TEAM ADVICE: This activity works well for remote teams. Use a remote board of your choice.

OPEN THE BOX 📶

Open the Box fosters innovation and challenges the current activities performed by the team.

1. Start by reading the following quote:

   "The world as we have created it is a process of our thinking. It cannot be changed without changing our thinking." – Albert Einstein.

2. Bring the participants' attention to the box metaphor (if possible, bring a box with you).

   "Inside this box there are all activities performed by the team. Please open the box..."

3. Split the whiteboard or canvas in three areas. Draw the open box in the center.

4. Explain each of the areas:
   * Which activities should be removed from the box?
   * Which activities should be added?
   * Which ones do we have to recycle?

We created this activity inspired by Silvio Meira's talk[13] on innovation. As he said, "sometimes we have to reinvent ourselves and think out of the box." It is an alternative to keep the team engaged while slightly changing the format.

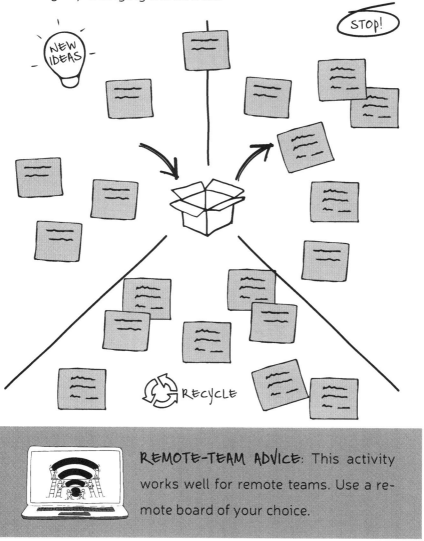

REMOTE-TEAM ADVICE: This activity works well for remote teams. Use a remote board of your choice.

---

[13] Available at: <http://www.youtube.com/watch?v=9q4vKRG5-0Q>. Access on: June, 2020.

THE STORY OF A STORY 📶

The Story of a Story targets process improvement by analyzing a work item's execution path (its story). We have used this activity for analyzing user stories[14] execution path. Please replace the word "story" for whatever work item with which you are working (e.g. feature request, bug ticket, order item).

RUNNING THE ACTIVITY:

1. Select a sample User Story (or a work item), describe it, and write it down on the top left corner of the canvas.
2. Write down the major events on its execution path (from inception to completion).
3. Write down the good things to repeat.
4. Write down the things to avoid, to be cautious about or consider changing.
5. Discuss with the group and use action items.

---

[14] COHN, Mike. *User Stories Applied: For Agile Software Development*. Addison-Wesley Professional, 2004.

This activity has a different structure from others. It focuses on one item and everything that happened to it. It pushes the team to reflect about concrete facts that happened and how they affected the outcome of a specific work item.

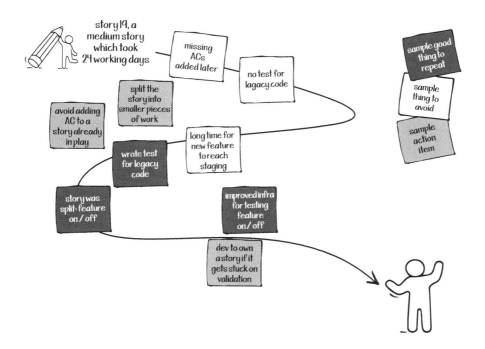

KNOWN ISSUES 🛜

Known Issues is a focused retrospective activity for issues that are already known. It is very useful for situations in which the team (1) either knows their issues and wants to talk about the solutions, or (2) keeps on running out of time to talk about repetitive issues that are not the top voted ones.

RUNNING THE ACTIVITY:

1. Split the participants into groups of two or three people.
2. Ask each group to write down the known issues.
3. Group the known issues and read them to the whole group.
4. Ask everyone to think about solutions to the known issues, write them on sticky notes (another color than the known issues) and place them next to the known issues.
5. Group conversation and action item creation.

The image illustrates this activity in action. On it, you can find the known issues categorized and grouped, as described on step 3, and the proposed solutions (on colored sticky notes), as described on step 4.

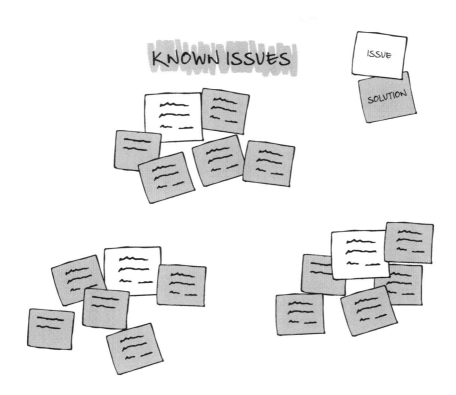

This activity was created by David Worthington.[15] He recommends running this activity followed by the Who-What-When check-out activity. We agree with David and find this activity very effective for project rescue situations, in which the issues list is well known.

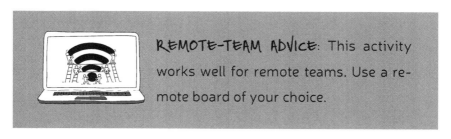

REMOTE-TEAM ADVICE: This activity works well for remote teams. Use a remote board of your choice.

---

[15] WORTHINGTON, David. *Reverse Retrospective*. Available at: <https://www.thought-works.com/insights/blog/reverse-retrospective-part-1>. Access on: May, 2020.

PROBLEMS & ACTIONS 🛜

Problems & Actions provides a quick way to brainstorm and select ideas and actions for solving problems affecting the team.

RUNNING THE ACTIVITY:

1. Ask participants to individually write down each and every perceived problem; one per sticky note.
2. Write the word problem on the top of the canvas, and then ask participants to place their sticky notes on that area. They should combine common notes.
3. Ask participants to individually write down all possible actions for solving those problems.
4. Write the word "actions" next to the word "problem" (on the top of the canvas), then ask participants to place their sticky notes on that area. They should combine common notes.
5. Have an open conversation about the problems and proposed actions.

This activity is especially useful, as it clearly separates the problems from the proposed actions toward solutions. It helps teams that typically go into solutions and lose context on which problem they are trying to solve. This activity can generate too many ideas, which might require further analysis and narrow down. Consider time-boxing it and planning a filtering activity after it.

PROBLEMS & ACTIONS

REMOTE-TEAM ADVICE: This activity works well for remote teams. Use a remote board of your choice.

THUMBS UP, THUMBS DOWN, NEW IDEAS AND ACKNOWLEDGEMENT 📶

Thumbs Up, Thumbs Down, New Ideas and Acknowledgement is great for bringing up new ideas and for acknowledging people and their efforts.

RUNNING THE ACTIVITY:

1. Split your canvas into four areas.
2. Explain each of the areas:
   * **Thumbs up:** things you like.
   * **Thumbs down:** things you dislike.
   * **New ideas:** new things to try.
   * **Acknowledgement:** appreciations/thank-yous.
3. Ask participants to share their notes.

This activity was loosely based on the Learning Matrix.[16] This is a common retrospective activity for data gathering. It is an alternative to keep the team engaged while slightly changing the format. One unique thing about it is the "acknowledgement" section: it is important for people to feel appreciated.

---

[16] LEUNG, H.Y. *Learning Matrix*. Available at: <http://cargocultism.wordpress.com/2010/10/08/learning-matrix/>. Access on: May, 2020.

REMOTE-TEAM ADVICE: This activity works well for remote teams. Use a remote board of your choice.

TIMELINE DRIVEN BY FEELINGS 📶

Timeline Driven by Feelings is a great retrospective activity to get the team thinking about events on a timeframe, and how they felt about them.

RUNNING THE ACTIVITY:

1. Draw the timeline.
2. Write a few events on the timeline (e.g. release started, high severity bug found in production, new person joined the team, a holiday).
3. Draw a happy face on the top, and a sad face on the bottom.
4. Ask participants to share their notes:

   "Please write down your notes, place the sticky note on the timeline canvas with relative horizontal position to the identified timeline events (as per step 2) and relative vertical position to how you felt about it (from super-happy to really sad, as per step 3)."

This activity is especially useful for getting people to open up and talk about their feelings, connecting them to actual data related to a period of time.

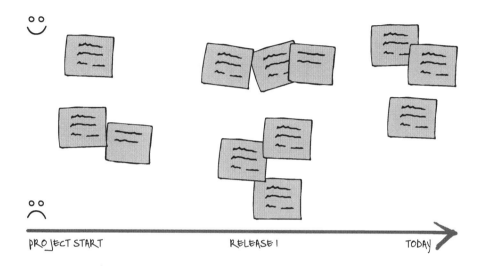

 **REMOTE-TEAM ADVICE:** This activity works well for remote teams. Use a remote board of your choice.

TIMELINE DRIVEN BY DATA 📶

Timeline Driven by Data is a great activity to get the team recollecting on events in a timeframe, with emphasis on different categories.

RUNNING THE ACTIVITY:

1. Start by creating a timeline at the bottom of the canvas.
2. Decide upon a few remarkable events to be added to the timeline (e.g.: project start date or a new person joining the team).
3. Create a few horizontal areas on the board, one for each category you want the team to focus on. For example, marketing, sales, support, engineering.
4. Ask participants to share their notes.
5. Discuss the notes and collect action items.

This activity helps the team think about different data points. By building a timeline, the team gets new insights based on actual data and how it affected the outcome.

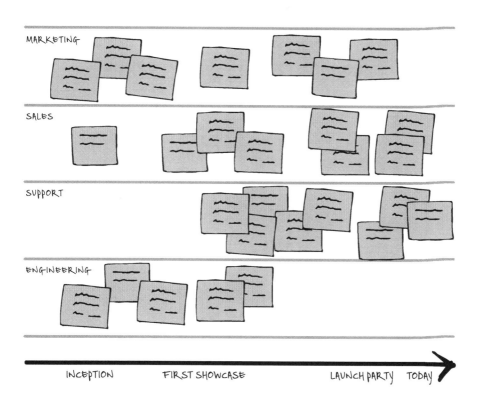

MARKETING

SALES

SUPPORT

ENGINEERING

INCEPTION   FIRST SHOWCASE   LAUNCH PARTY TODAY

REMOTE-TEAM ADVICE: This activity works well for remote teams. Use a remote board of your choice.

FUTURE DIRECTION, LESSONS LEARNED, ACCOMPLISHMENTS AND PROBLEM AREAS (FLAP) 🛜

FLAP is a great project/phase postmortem activity. You should run it as close to the end of a project/phase as possible—don't wait or everyone will forget what happened.

RUNNING THE ACTIVITY:

1. Prepare and explain the FLAP canvas quadrants:
   * **Future directions:** Please write down all future directions regarding the project/phase.
   * **Lessons learned:** Please write down the key lessons and takeaways from the project/phase.
   * **Accomplishments:** Please write down the key accomplishments for the project/phase.
   * **Problem areas:** Please write down the problematic areas experienced throughout the specified project/phase.
2. Ask participants for their notes.
3. Discuss with the group and share the results.

This activity is a change for the usual retrospective, covering a broader area and looking ahead. It gets the team reflecting about what happened and how those lessons can be applied in future projects. It also provides a space for the team to celebrate their achievements.

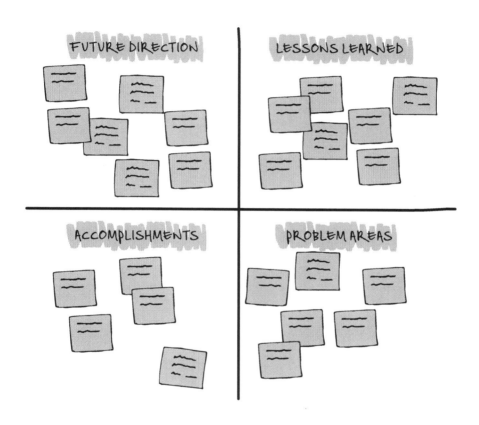

FUTURE DIRECTION

LESSONS LEARNED

ACCOMPLISHMENTS

PROBLEM AREAS

REMOTE-TEAM ADVICE: This activity works well for remote teams. Use a remote board of your choice.

DEALING WITH FAILURE - FMEA 📶

Dealing with Failure is an application of FMEA,[17] a design tool used to systematically analyze postulated failures and identify actions and verifications. It is appropriate for a target retrospective focused on a failure.

RUNNING THE ACTIVITY:

1. Explain the failure under analysis (summarize it on top of the canvas).

2. Split the canvas into the following four areas: analysis, evaluation, action, verification.

   * **Analysis:** What is the failure? What led to it?

   * **Evaluation:** What are the consequences of this failure? What is its severity? What is the probability that it will happen again?

   * **Action:** What are the corrective and preventive actions (so it does not happen again) for this failure?

   * **Verification:** Given the listed actions, how can we verify their outcome?

3. Split the team into smaller groups (two or three people each).

4. For each of the four areas, give a few minutes for writing notes (smaller group), followed by a few minutes for a group conversation.

---

[17] TAGUE, Nancy. *Quality Toolbox*. ASQ Quality Press, 2005.

This is a very focused activity, looking only into one specific problem/failure and what the team should do to handle the consequences, work on corrective actions, and verify their result.

FAILURE: Customers unable to complete purchase

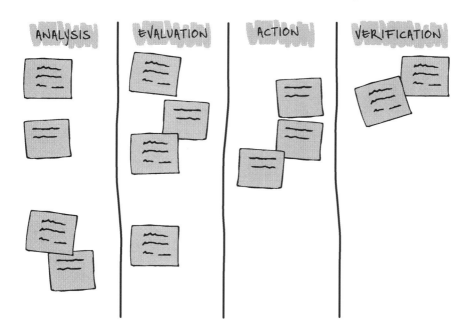

REMOTE-TEAM ADVICE: This activity works well for remote teams. Use a remote board of your choice.

DAKI - DROP, ADD, KEEP, IMPROVE 🛜

DAKI is a great data-gathering activity to foster the thinking around practices and the value the team gets from them. It helps team members understand each other's perceived value on such practices.

RUNNING THE ACTIVITY:

1. Divide the canvas in four quadrants: Drop, Add, Keep, Improve.
2. Ask participants for their notes.
3. Group the notes and discuss.

This is a common retrospective activity for data gathering. It is an alternative to keep the team engaged while slightly changing the format.

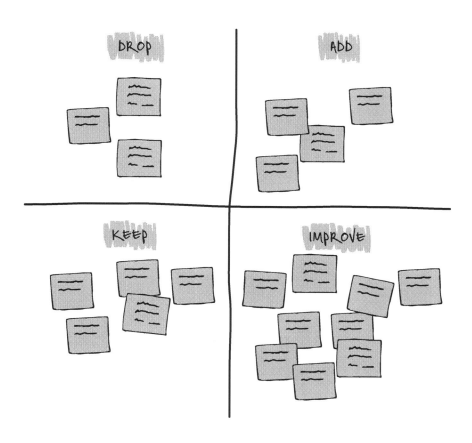

REMOTE-TEAM ADVICE: This activity works well for remote teams. Use a remote board of your choice.

THE 3LS: LIKED, LEARNED, LACKED 🛜

The 3Ls is a great data gathering activity, especially for retrospectives for a longer period of time.

1. Split the canvas in three areas:
   * **Liked** – things you really liked.
   * **Learned** – things you have learned.
   * **Lacked** – things you wish had happened.
2. Ask participants to individually write notes on sticky notes for each of the areas.
3. Discuss with the group about the notes.

This activity is inspired by the 4Ls activity.[18] It is a common retrospective activity for data gathering. It is an alternative to keep the team engaged while slightly changing the format.

---

[18] GORMAN, Mary; GOTTESDIENER, Ellen. *The 4Ls retrospective technique*. Available at: <http://ebgconsulting.com/blog/the-4l%E2%80%99s-a-retrospective-technique/>. Access on: December, 2013.

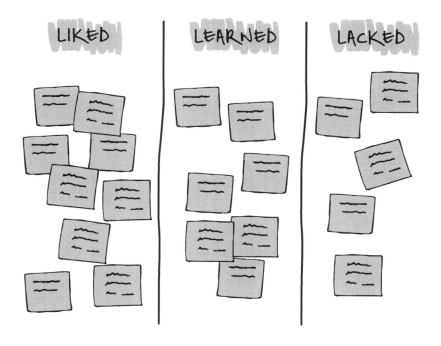

REMOTE-TEAM ADVICE: This activity works well for remote teams. Use a remote board of your choice.

STARFISH ⋯

Starfish is a great data-gathering activity to foster the thinking around practices and the value the team gets from them. It helps team members understand each other's perceived value on such practices.

RUNNING THE ACTIVITY:

1. Split the canvas in five areas:
   * **Keep doing** – something the team is doing well and whose value you acknowledge.
   * **Less of** – something already being done; you see some value, but would rather cut down a little bit.
   * **More of** – something already being done which you believe will bring more value if done even more.
   * **Stop doing** – something that is not adding value or, even worse, is getting on the way.
   * **Start doing** – a new idea or something you have seen working before that you would like to bring to the table.
2. Ask participants to individually write notes on sticky notes for each of the areas.
3. Discuss with the group about the notes.

We have learned this activity from Pat Kua.[19] This is a common retrospective activity for data gathering. It is an alternative to keep the team engaged while slightly changing the format. A very common variation is to have three areas: keep doing, less of, and more of.

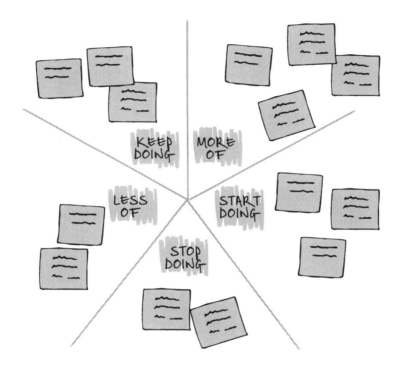

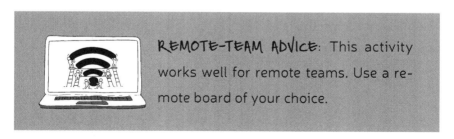

REMOTE-TEAM ADVICE: This activity works well for remote teams. Use a remote board of your choice.

[19] KUA, Patrick. *The Retrospective Starfish*. Available at: <https://www.thekua.com/rant/2006/03/the-retrospective-starfish/>. Access on: May, 2020.

LESSONS LEARNED - PLANNED vs. SUCCESS 📶

Lessons Learned is a great retrospective activity for analyzing an event or a period of time and looking at the data from the perspective of plan and success.

RUNNING THE ACTIVITY:

1. Draw the canvas with a horizontal arrow with "Planned" on the left and "Unplanned" on the right, as well as a vertical arrow crossing it with "Failure" at the bottom and "Success" at the top.

2. Ask participants to write their notes:

   "The bigger the success, the higher you should place your note (failures go to the lower part of the canvas). If you consider your note is about something highly planned, then place it on the very left; otherwise you should place it on the right side of the canvas."

3. Discuss with the group.

This activity discloses the correlation (or absence of correlation) between planning and succeeding. Sometimes there are things that are highly planned but still go wrong, while other times there are things that the team did not even think about previously go really well.

The final result depicts four quadrants: planned and successful; unintended and successful; planned but failed; and failed and not planned. The conversation about each of these quadrants brings visibility and areas for improvement, as well as a chance of recognizing what worked well (even if it was not planned!).

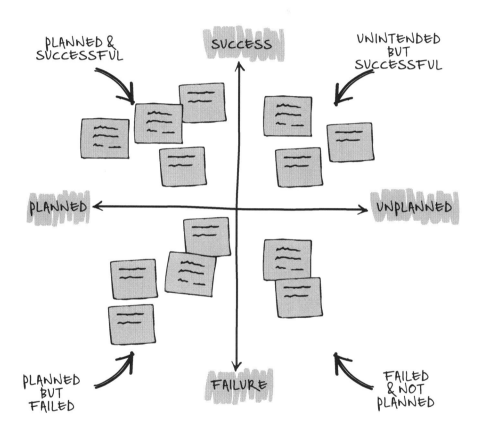

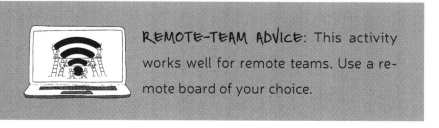

REMOTE-TEAM ADVICE: This activity works well for remote teams. Use a remote board of your choice.

PLEASURE AND GAIN 📶

Pleasure and Gain is great for talking about all work-related things and how they affect each participant (in relation to being pleasant or not), and how much gain they bring to the team.

1. Draw the pleasure and gain graph.
2. Instruct participants to add notes to the graph: "Of the things you do at work, please answer the following questions:
   * Do you have pleasure or feel pain for doing such things?
   * How much gain or loss do you get by doing such things?"
3. Explain to participants about the magic quadrant, the pleasure and gain quadrant, and the Big Pain intersection.
4. Hold a conversation about what could be done so we move each item towards the magic quadrant.

This activity is based on the psychologist Daniel Kahneman's Loss Aversion Theory.[20] The theory findings indicate the pain of losing is psychologically almost two times as powerful as the pleasure of gaining. This activity fosters very important conversations that can change a team.

---

[20] TVERSKY, Amos. KAHNEMAN, Daniel. *Loss Aversion in Riskless Choice: A Reference Dependent Model.* Quarterly Journal of Economics, 1991.

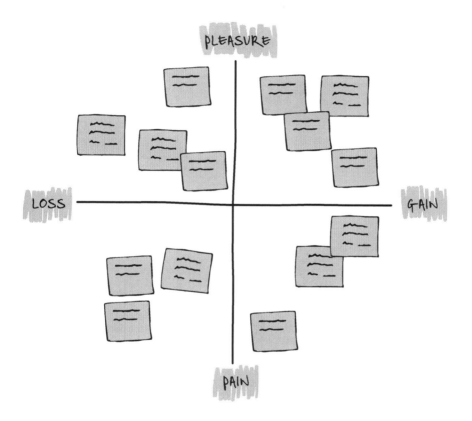

 **REMOTE-TEAM ADVICE**: This activity works well for remote teams. Use a remote board of your choice.

THREE LITTLE PIGS 📶

Three Little Pigs is a fun retrospective activity that uses the Three Little Pigs story to foster a conversation about improvements for making our structures more solid.

RUNNING THE ACTIVITY:

1. Draw and explain the three columns to participants:
   * **House of straw:** What do we do that just about hangs together, but could topple over at any minute? (E.g. "our deployment script is very manual, and prone to error—we could break production very easily.")
   * **House of sticks:** What do we do that is pretty solid, but could be improved? (E.g. "our automated tests are pretty good, but sometimes they fail for no reason, and we have to run them again, which is a pain.")
   * **House of bricks:** What do we do that is rock solid? (E.g. "our automated deployment has never failed. It rocks.")
2. Ask participants to share their comments on sticky notes and place them on one of the three columns.
3. Filter and group conversation about action items.

It is an awesome and fun activity, especially when it involves a good drawing of the three pigs with their houses. It is a good activity for data gathering and works well as an alternative to keep the team engaged while slightly changing the format.

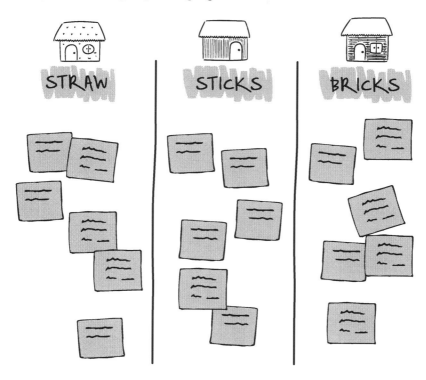

REMOTE-TEAM ADVICE: This activity works well for remote teams. Use a remote board of your choice.

ERROR CONVERSATION 📶

Error Conversation helps the team identify errors, understand their nature and have a productive conversation about them. It is especially useful for a team dealing with many errors over a period of time.

RUNNING THE ACTIVITY:

1. Start by asking everyone to individually list all the errors that occurred for the given period (e.g., "write on sticky notes and keep them until the next step").

2. Draw and explain the board with two columns for two types of error:
   * **Error of commission:** errors of commission are errors that occurred because of doing something that should not have been done.
   * **Error of omission:** errors of omission are errors that occurred because of not doing something that should have been done.

3. Ask someone to share one error and place it on the appropriate column.

4. Have a brief conversation about the error. Consider doing affinity grouping by adding similar notes to it. Consider writing notes and action items on separate sticky notes (preferably of a different color) and placing next to the related error.

5. Go to the next errors until all notes are finished or you run out of time.

This activity is inspired by the book *Re-Creating the Corporation: A Design of Organizations for the 21st Century.*[21] In it, the author elaborates that there are two possible types of decision-making mistakes: errors of commission and errors of omission. This activity helps the group talk and address those.

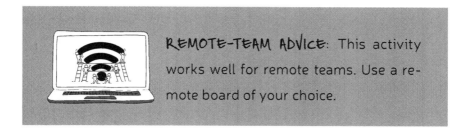

REMOTE-TEAM ADVICE: This activity works well for remote teams. Use a remote board of your choice.

---

[21] ACKOFF, Russell L. *Re-Creating the Corporation: A Design of Organizations for the 21st Century.* Oxford University Press, 1999.

MAIN COURSE: FUTERESPECTIVES, LOOKING AHEAD

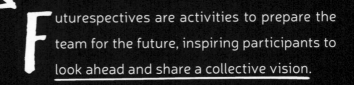

Futurespectives are activities to prepare the team for the future, inspiring participants to look ahead and share a collective vision.

HOPES AND CONCERNS 🛜

Hopes and Concerns is a great activity for getting people to open up and share their feelings about what's ahead.

RUNNING THE ACTIVITY:

1. Draw a vertical line on a canvas, splitting it on two sides with the titles: Hopes and Concerns.
2. Ask participants to write down on a sticky note their hopes and concerns for what's ahead (an event, workshop, next release, new project etc.).
3. Group conversation about the notes.

This activity is especially useful for getting people to open up and talk about their feelings regarding something that is about to happen; therefore, it is a futurespective activity. Consider revisiting the hopes and concerns over time to verify if they are being addressed.

REMOTE-TEAM ADVICE: This activity works well for remote teams. Use a remote board of your choice.

PLAN OF ACTION 📶

Plan of Action raises the participant's most appealing ideas. It brings a good balance on time and collaboration while encouraging participants to discuss and sign up to actionable work.

RUNNING THE ACTIVITY:

1. Ask participants to individually write actions on the specific format below. Each participant should write from one to three actions on index cards:
    *   **Long-term goal:** what is the long-term goal for this idea?
    *   **Now-action:** the very first concrete action toward the goal.

2. Split the large group into smaller groups.
3. Ask the groups to decide upon the top two cards.
4. Join two adjacent groups and repeat the step above.
5. Repeat steps 3 and 4 if desirable (depends on the group size and if you want fewer selected cards/actions).
6. Ask participants to present each of the selected top cards to the whole group.
7. Ask each person to write down their name on a small sticky note and place it on the card they want to work on.

This activity is especially useful for motivating large groups of people to: (1) elaborate goals and identify concrete actionable work items, and (2) to coordinate and collaborate upon the execution of concrete action items.

Plan of Action[22] follows the same structure as described in the 1-2-4-All activity in Liberating Structures.[23]

PLAN OF ACTION

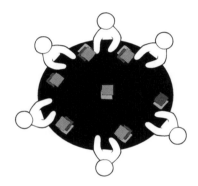

Long term goal: ———————
Now action: ～～～～～

 REMOTE-TEAM ADVICE: This activity works well for remote teams. Use the team's remote communication tool to pair up participants in separate chat rooms, then bring participants together incrementally until the whole group is in the same room again.

[22] LARMAN, Craig; VODDE, Bas. *Practices for Scaling Lean & Agile Development: Large, Multisite, and Offshore Product Development with Large-Scale Scrum*. Addison-Wesley Professional, 2010.

[23] LIPMANOWICZ, Henri; MCCANDLESS, KEITH. *The Surprising Power of Liberating Structures: Simple Rules to Unleash A Culture of Innovation*. Liberating Structures Press, 2014.

PATH TO NIRVANA 📶

Path to Nirvana is a great activity that focuses on creating a common goal alignment and visualizing smaller steps toward a big achievement.

RUNNING THE ACTIVITY:

This activity is divided into two parts.

Part one – defining nirvana

1. Write the word "nirvana" on the top right corner of the canvas.
2. Break the team into smaller groups of three or four people each.
3. Ask each group to write a short sentence to describe the nirvana.
4. Each group presents its short sentence describing the nirvana.
5. Create one common sentence to define nirvana.

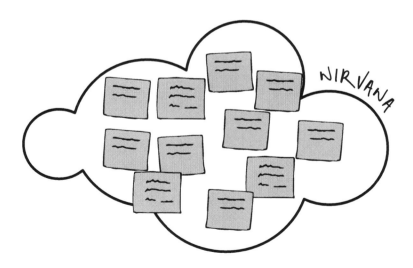

Part two – path to nirvana

1. Write the word "nirvana" on the top right corner of the canvas, with its definition.

2. Draw a timeline on the canvas, having the word "today" on the leftmost side.

3. Write down major events or time periods on the timeline (e.g., Christmas holidays, Summer school vacation, July, month one, month six...).

4. Ask participants to add notes for smaller steps on the path to nirvana.

5. Group conversation about the steps.

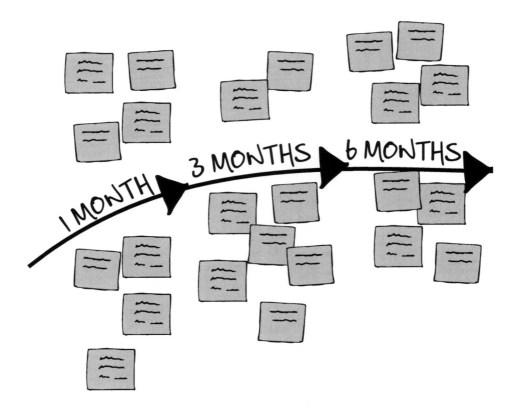

It is very interesting to see how this simple question gets partici-pants very engaged and then aligned: what is our nirvana? Once the team is in agreement about that, it's much easier to clarify the steps towards it.

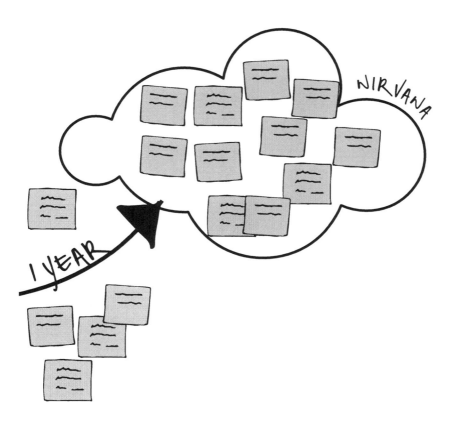

 REMOTE-TEAM ADVICE: This activity works well for remote teams. Use a re-mote board of your choice.

PRE-MORTEM ACTIVITY 🤶

The **Pre-Mortem Activity** is great in preparing for an upcoming release or challenge. With a different perspective, the activity guides participants to talk about all that could go wrong. Then, the conversation switches to a mitigation and action plan.

RUNNING THE ACTIVITY:

1. Draw the pre-mortem canvas with the main topic for discussion: what will go wrong? How will this end in disaster?
2. Ask participants to individually write down risks and concerns.
3. Coordinate participants to add their notes to the canvas.
4. Add a new theme color for mitigation and ask participants to write down notes related to how to mitigate the risks and concerns.
5. Discuss with the group and make a plan of action.

It is common for teams to do a post-mortem activity after something goes wrong. But it is much better to avoid anything from going wrong in the first place. This activity brings structure to think about and prepare for possible problems.

REMOTE-TEAM ADVICE: This activity works well for remote teams. Use a remote board of your choice.

SPEED CAR - ABYSS 📶

Speed Car — Abyss is a forward-thinking exercise, with an eye on the past. It is a mix of retrospective and futurespective, which uncovers risks.

RUNNING THE ACTIVITY:

1. Draw the picture below in a common canvas.
2. Ask participants to share their notes for each of the retrospective areas:

   "Let's start by looking back. Please, write notes and place them on the following two areas on the left side of the drawing: engine and parachute."

   * **Looking back** — engine: what has been pushing us forward? Making us move fast?
   * **Looking back** — parachute: what has been slowing us down?
3. Ask participants to share their notes, thinking about the future.

   "Now, let's look ahead at the near future. Please, write notes and place them on the following two areas on the right side of the drawing: abyss and bridge."

   * **Looking ahead** — abyss: what are the dangers ahead? What could take us down the road?
   * **Looking ahead** — bridge: what could we build to overcome such challenges? What shall we do to overcome the abyss?
4. Group notes and debate.

Sometimes we need an activity to look at the past and the future at the same time, so that the discussion is not only about fixing what went wrong: it is also about preparing for what's ahead.

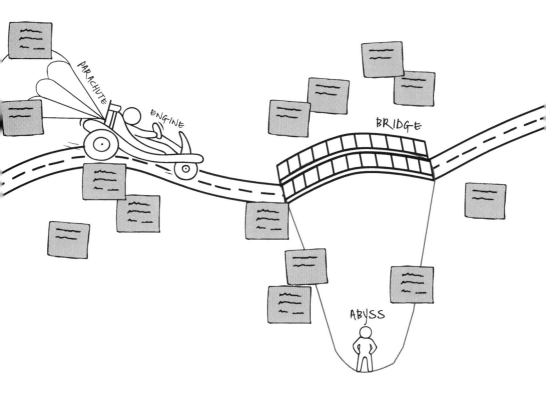

REMOTE-TEAM ADVICE: This activity works well for remote teams. Use a remote board of your choice.

HOT-AIR BALLOON - BAD WEATHER ᗆ

Hot-air Balloon — Bad Weather is a forward-thinking exercise, with an eye on the past. It is a mix of retrospective and futurespective, which uncovers risks.

RUNNING THE ACTIVITY:

1. Draw a hot-air balloon in a common canvas.
2. Ask participants to share their notes for each of the retrospective areas.

   "Let's start by looking back. Please, write notes and place them on the following two areas above and below the balloon: hot-air and sand-bags."

   * **Looking back** — fire and hot-air: what helps us go higher? What are the things that push us forward?
   * **Looking back** — forces pulling down: which are the forces pulling us down?
3. Ask participants to share their notes, thinking about the future.

   "Now, let's look ahead, at the near future. Please, write notes and place them on the following two areas on both sides of the balloon: storm and sunny day."

   * **Looking ahead** — storm: what is the storm ahead of us? What will make our trip turbulent?

* **Looking ahead** – sunny day: what could we do to avoid the storm and turn toward sunny days? What shall we do to overcome the possible challenges ahead of us?

4. Gather up group notes and discuss.

Different people prefer different analogies. Some will prefer a balloon, others a speed-car. The important thing is to use a simple and effective analogy to get the participation and the ideas flowing.

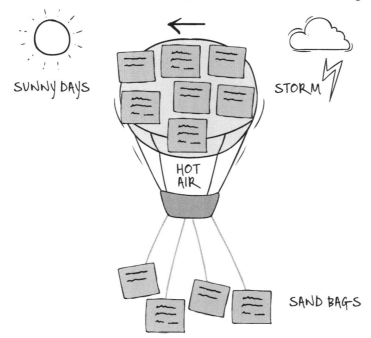

SUNNY DAYS   STORM

HOT AIR

SAND BAGS

REMOTE-TEAM ADVICE: This activity works well for remote teams. Use a remote board of your choice.

FUTURE FACEBOOK POSTS 🛜

Future Facebook Posts is an activity that gets the team thinking about possible future events with a positive mindset, as typically people share good things in social media.

RUNNING THE ACTIVITY:

1. Start by introducing the activity:

"Please, assume everyone on the team would be posting on Facebook and imagine you will travel in time and be able to look at our team timeline (with all posts)."

2. Ask participants to write down future Facebook posts (individually):

"Please, write down (individually) your Facebook posts in the future. These posts should have a short text and a date in the future (e.g., the release date)."

3. Place the posts visible on a timeline.

4. Ask participants to add up to five "likes" to all the posts.

5. Discuss with the group and create action items.

Similar options are Future Twitter Posts, focusing on short sentences; or Future Instagram Posts, where participants have to share drawings with text, which gets even more engaging and fun. A good add-on is to add more reactions (hearts, laugh, smiling face…), to make the team's feelings towards those future events surface.

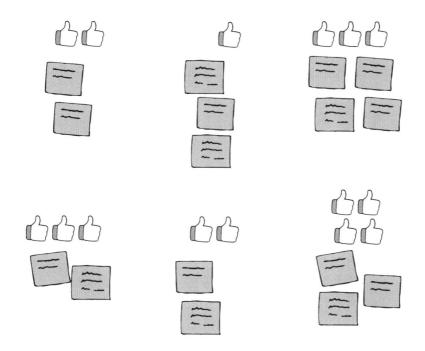

REMOTE-TEAM ADVICE: This activity works well for remote teams. Use a remote board of your choice.

PMI – PLUS, MINUS, INTERESTING 📶

PMI is a futurespective for discussing an idea or concept from multiple points of view. It fosters conversations about the positive (plus), negative (minus), and considerations that are neither good nor bad (interesting).

RUNNING THE ACTIVITY:

1. Split the canvas into three areas: plus, minus, interesting.
2. Ask participants to add notes to each area: "What do you consider will be positive (plus), negative (minus) and interesting about what's ahead of us."
3. Discuss with the group about the notes.

The PMI thinking activity was developed by Dr. Edward de Bono,[24] father of lateral thinking and creativity. While it works well for looking ahead, we have also seen it working well as a retrospective. In this case, change the sentence to "please share with us what you consider was the positive (plus), negative (minus), or interesting".

---

[24] DE BONO, Edward. Tactics: *The Art and Science of Success*. Gardners Books, 1995.

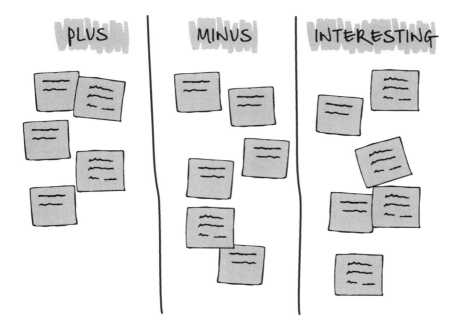

REMOTE-TEAM ADVICE: This activity works well for remote teams. Use a remote board of your choice.

RISK BRAINSTORMING AND MITIGATION 📶

Risk Brainstorming and Mitigation is a collective thinking activity to develop the team criticisms, awareness, and responsiveness for possible challenges ahead of it.

RUNNING THE ACTIVITY:

1. Draw the canvas for the activity, as shown in the picture below.
2. Ask participants to identify possible risks:

   "Write down things that can negatively impact our project. Place it on the top of the canvas."
3. For the identified risks, ask participants to discuss and add notes in the following order:

   * **Prevention** – What is in place that will attempt to stop the risk happening in the first place? (E.g., security, awareness & training programs, qualified staff, planning, and/or procedures.)

   * **Detection** – What is in place that will let me know if and when the risk does happen? (E.g., staff/customer reporting mechanisms, financial reconciliation, fire alarms, audits.)

   * **Response** – If the risk happens anyway, what measures do we have in place to lessen the impact? (E.g., contingency plans, backups, insurance, resolution processes.)

Every team needs to think about risks and how to mitigate them. Instead of just listing risks and thinking about mitigation steps, this activity adds other aspects to it—how to prevent it in the first place, detect it if it happens, and define what the team's response should be. It is a collaborative activity where the whole team has a chance to contribute with ideas.

RISK: Integration with external systems will not work as expected

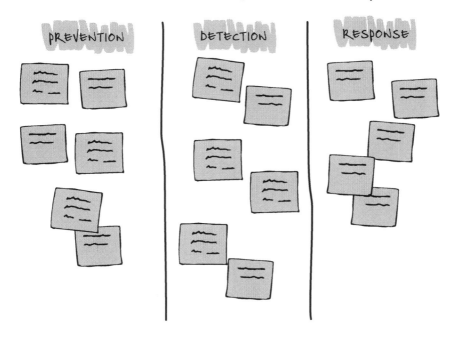

 REMOTE-TEAM ADVICE: This activity works well for remote teams. Use a remote board of your choice.

LETTERS TO THE FUTURE 📶

The Letters to the Future activity is appropriate for when the team needs to look ahead and think about the future, thinking about what they expect to happen in a given time frame.

RUNNING THE ACTIVITY:

1. Ask participants to think about the given context and to individually choose a person for whom they would like to send a letter in the future (it can be the product owner, project manager, another team member; whoever they think is appropriate).

2. Ask participants to individually write a short letter to that person, saying whatever they want. The letter should have a date in the future.

3. Read the letters out loud, discuss, and consider keeping them for the future.

Leaving the addressee open will give space for each participant to send the letter to different people. Some will send it to the company's CEO, others will think about a manager, and some may send the letter to the team. The diversity of addressees, dates, and letter content uncovers different perspectives for the team's future.

REMOTE-TEAM ADVICE: This activity works well for remote teams. Ask participants to write the letter in their favorite text editor, share it with everyone else, and save it for future reference.

RAID - RISKS, ASSUMPTIONS, ISSUES AND DEPENDENCIES 🛜

The **RAID** activity helps a team have a conversation about risks and issues, assumptions, and dependencies. These are very important aspects, especially when looking ahead and preparing for the future.

RUNNING THE ACTIVITY:

1. Prepare the RAID canvas with the following four areas: risks, assumptions, issues and dependencies.
2. Ask participants to write down their comments on individual sticky notes for each of the four areas.
3. Conversation and action items about the notes.

Sometimes, participants will ask about the difference between risk and issue. A risk is something that might become a problem. An issue is already a problem. Another common situation is the feeling that a note might belong on more than one quadrant. In such cases, instruct participants to write more than one note, each one specifically to the quadrant. For instance: (dependency) "integration with system ABC for the Single Sign On feature", and (risk) "Single Sign On integration effort being much bigger than originally accounted for".

An open conversation about the four quadrants in this activity brings visibility and alignment to the team, so that it has a higher chance of success in the future.

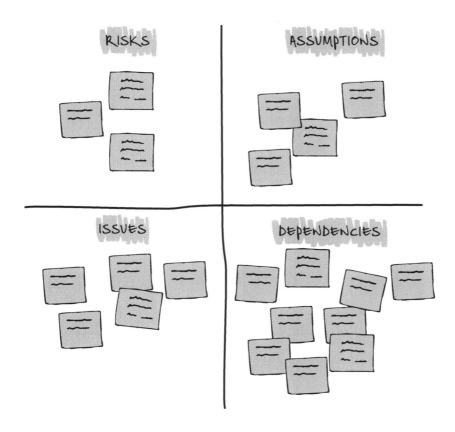

REMOTE-TEAM ADVICE: This activity works well for remote teams. Use a remote board of your choice.

THE CATAPULT 🛜

The Catapult is great for planning and preparing for an upcoming challenge. With a simple metaphor, this activity guides participants to look at the challenge from three perspectives: the person facing the challenge, the challenge itself, and people's organization to overcome the challenge.

RUNNING THE ACTIVITY:

1. Draw a catapult with a person flying and a mountain ahead.
2. Ask participants to write notes for each of the three areas:
   * **The catapult:** notes related to the organization people engage in to overcome the challenge.
   * **Person flying:** notes related to the person facing the challenge.
   * **Mountain:** the challenge itself.
3. Conversation about the notes. Consider guiding the conversation by connecting related notes from the three areas.

Note on the image the nirvana behind the mountain (colored sticky notes at the right side of the picture). The catapult activity builds up on the assumption that people are trying to reach the magic place, the nirvana, and as such it helps the team find out the steps to get there. If the nirvana is not clear, consider running the first part of the Path to Nirvana activity.

We recommend that you play this YouTube video[25] as an opening bang for this activity.

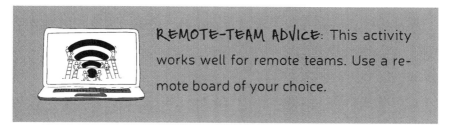

REMOTE-TEAM ADVICE: This activity works well for remote teams. Use a remote board of your choice.

---

[25] Available at: <www.caroli.org/human-catapult/>. Access on: June, 2020.

SUCCESS CRITERIA 📶

The **Success Criteria** for a team should be brief, succinct, with clearly defined intentions, target outcome, and conditions for proving its results. This activity helps the team align on that.

1. Create a canvas with the following labels:
   * **Intention:** the idea that you plan (or intend) to carry out.
   * **Target:** the key target outcomes towards the intention.
   * **Successful if:** the indicator(s) that prove(s) the criteria is being met.
   * **Failure if:** the indicator(s) that prove(s) the criteria is not being met.
2. Write down the intention (consider defining it as a group if it is not clearly stated).
3. Ask participants to write down the key target outcomes towards the intention on individual sticky notes.
4. Place notes on the target area.
5. Organize the target outcomes. Consider grouping similar notes and removing or rewriting notes that are not clear or broadly defined.
6. Ask participants to write and place notes for each target outcome for the success and failure indication condition. Place these on the same line as the target outcome.
7. Group conversation about the notes on each line.

A clear success criteria for a team leads to more focused actions to achieve it. This activity helps the team be on the same page for what the criteria is, and how they will track its progress.

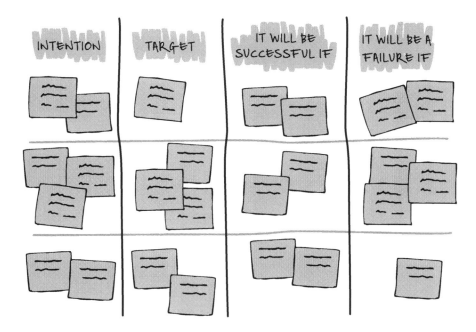

REMOTE-TEAM ADVICE: This activity works well for remote teams. Use a remote board of your choice.

HERO'S JOURNEY 📶

Hero's Journey is a futurespective activity to help describe a story that the team is pursuing.

RUNNING THE ACTIVITY:

1. Explain the intention of the activity: "We are here to collectively write our hero's journey story."
2. Describe the main areas of your journey. We are focusing on the following areas of our story:
   * **The hero:** the person or group going through the journey.
   * **The guide:** the people and things guiding the hero.
   * **The cavern:** the challenges ahead.
   * **The treasure:** the awards and achievements.
3. Ask participants to write their notes for each area.
4. Group conversation.

We have applied this activity for describing what a large organization transformation would be like. It was very helpful for early identification of the people involved, the main challenges, desired outcomes, and needed guidance. We have also seen it being used after the fact, not as a futurespective, but as an activity to help the team tell a story about a journey they have just gone through.

This activity is inspired by Joseph Campbell's book,[26] which also inspired many movies, books, tv shows etc. You could play a video[27] about heroes before starting the activity, getting the team into the activity's mindset.

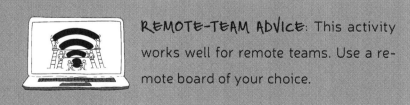

REMOTE-TEAM ADVICE: This activity works well for remote teams. Use a remote board of your choice.

---

[26] CAMPBELL, Joseph. *The Hero with a Thousand Faces*. New World Library, 2008.

[27] Available at: <caroli.org/hero-journey>. Access on: June, 2020.

FILTERING

When a lot of data is generated by any activity, it is important to have well-defined criteria to decide what will be discussed. Given the meeting's limited time, it is possible that topics will be left out of the debate.

DOT VOTING �ᯤ

Dot Voting is a great activity for time management and prioritization. It is typically used for focusing the conversation on fewer items with highest interest by the group.

RUNNING THE ACTIVITY:

1. Instruct participants on the voting rules:
   * Each participant is entitled to five votes (each vote will be represented by a dot on the sticky note).
   * Participants can place more than one vote on a card.
2. Go vote!

   "Please, vote on the items that you want to debate. The items with most votes will be picked up first."
3. Engage on a group conversation following the group's interest rank (most voted items first).

This is a simple way to prioritize items for discussion. In retrospectives, it is common to generate a lot of insights. While all of them are valuable, time is limited, and therefore you need to make choices on what to discuss. Dot voting gives a chance for all participants to vote on what they consider most important to talk about.

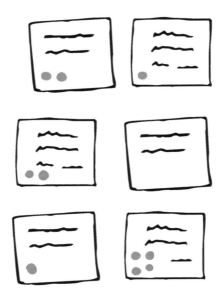

 REMOTE-TEAM ADVICE: If the remote board of your choice supports voting, use that feature. If it does not, you can ask participants to add "+1" or another mark of your choice in the sticky notes.

SELECT ONE AND TALK 📶

Select One and Talk helps filter and manage time while a group of people has conversations about several items of a (large) list. It is a good alternative for dot voting or some other style of group voting, to filter the conversation to fewer items.

RUNNING THE ACTIVITY:

1. Decide the order in which participants will talk (e.g., name alphabetic order, age order or position order—from left to right).
2. Decide the limit of time for each item conversation (e.g., at most three minutes per item conversation) and the activity time (e.g., thirty minutes).
3. The first person chooses an item, reads it out loud, then the group has a conversation about it.
4. Go to the next person/conversation until the activity time is over or all items have been covered.

This activity promotes a faster option for filtering, as it does not require time for voting. It also brings a different perspective to the group dynamic, as it fosters a conversation about what is important to each person.

At times, some people feel frustrated because a specific topic has not been selected for conversation. This typically happens because of voting systems. This activity addresses such situations, allowing individuals to select a topic which is important to them.

REMOTE-TEAM ADVICE: This activity works well for remote teams. Share a remote board with the participants, then ask everyone to enter their name. Organize the names in a sequence and follow it for the activity.

PLUS MINUS VOTING ⌗

Plus Minus Voting is a great activity for time management and prioritization. It is typically used for focusing the conversation on fewer items of the group's highest interest.

RUNNING THE ACTIVITY:

1. Instruct the participant on the voting rules:
   * Each participant is entitled to three +s and three -s votes (each vote will be represented by a + or − mark on the sticky note).
   * Participants can place more than one vote on a card.
   * (+) represents your agreement with a note and that you want to talk about it.
   * (−) represents your disagreement with a note and that you want to talk about it

   "Please, vote on the items that you want to discuss. The items with the most votes will be picked up first."
2. Go vote!
3. Engage on a group conversation following the group's interest rank (notes with most marks first).

This is a variation of the Dot Voting activity which allows participants to be clearer about agreements and disagreements. You can also change it up so that participants put a "thumbs up" or a "thumbs down."

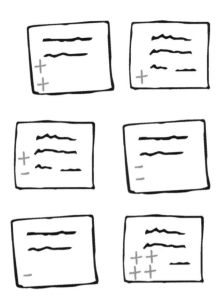

REMOTE-TEAM ADVICE: If the remote board of your choice supports voting, use that feature. If it does not, you can ask participants to add "+"and "-" to the sticky notes.

TELL AND CLUSTER 📶

Tell and Cluster is an easy and effective way to get individual notes clustered on affinity groups.

RUNNING THE ACTIVITY:

1. Ask a participant to choose one note and read it out loud.
2. Ask the other participants if they have similar notes. If they do, ask them to read them and place them (cluster) next to the first one on that affinity group.
3. Ask any participant to share a new note and then place it on the canvas starting a new cluster.
4. Go back to step 2 until all notes are gone.

By the end of this activity, similar notes should be grouped, making the similarities visual and highlighting recurring themes. Focus the conversation on the clusters with more notes.

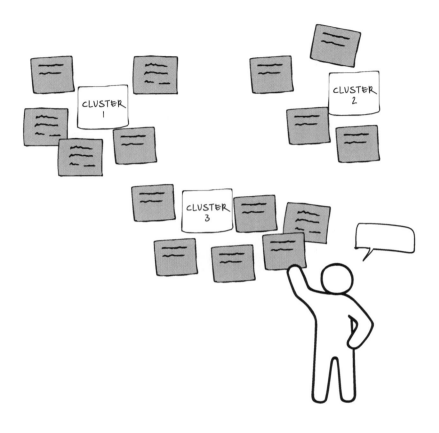

 **REMOTE-TEAM ADVICE**: This activity works well for remote teams. Use a remote board of your choice. Ask participants first to write their notes individually and then cluster them as they are presented.

FISHBOWL CONVERSATION 🛜

Fishbowl Conversation is great for keeping a focused conversation when you have a large group of people. At any time, only a few people have a conversation (the fish in the fishbowl). The remaining people are listeners (the ones watching the fishbowl). The caveat is that the listeners can join the discussion at any moment.

RUNNING THE ACTIVITY:

1. Place five chairs in an open area facing each other. The chairs should be in the middle of the room, or around a round table.

2. Instruct participants on the fishbowl rules:

   "Four people should sit on the chairs. They will start the conversation. One chair is to be kept empty all the time. It is available for whoever wants to join the conversation. When someone sits on the empty chair, someone else (typically the one either sitting longer or less involved in the current conversation) has to leave, vacating one chair.

   The other participants who are not sitting on the fishbowl chairs cannot get involved in the conversation. They are listeners. If they are to speak, they first have to sit on the empty chair."

3. Select a topic for the fishbowl conversation and get started.

4. Switch topics whenever appropriate. It can be time-boxed or changed whenever the conversation runs out.

We have seen this activity being used in conferences and large group conversations. We find it especially useful for very large group conversations, with pre-selected topics.

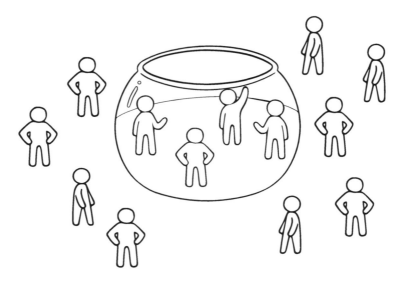

 REMOTE-TEAM ADVICE: This activity works well for remote teams. Use a remote board of your choice. Write the name of each participant on a sticky note and define the fishbowl area. The sticky notes in that area represent the talking fish in the fishbowl and should be moved accordingly as people enter and leave the conversation.

FEASIBLE X USEFUL 📶

Feasible x Useful provides a fast way to prioritize a list of items by relatively comparing levels of feasibility and how useful each item is.

RUNNING THE ACTIVITY:

1. Draw the Feasible x Useful graph and place the items from the previous activity near it.
2. Ask participants to grade each item and place them in the graph, positioned accordingly:
   * **Feasible:** Can it be done? How realistic is it?
   * **Useful:** Does the item actually solve the problem? How effective will it be?
3. Identify the top ranked items (highly feasible and useful) as the ones that will be tackled by the team.

By the end of this activity, the items considered to be highly feasible and useful will be visible to everyone. These should take priority amongst all the items. Most likely, items that have low feasibility and are not considered too useful are discarded.

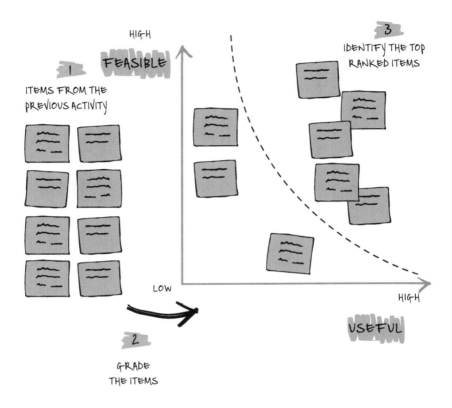

HIGH

FEASIBLE

1
ITEMS FROM THE
PREVIOUS ACTIVITY

3
IDENTIFY THE TOP
RANKED ITEMS

LOW

HIGH

USEFUL

2
GRADE
THE ITEMS

REMOTE-TEAM ADVICE: This activity works well for remote teams. Use a remote board that allows the input to be moved freely. After participants add their notes to the main course activity, ask them to move their notes to the graph area as they filter it.

LIKELIHOOD X IMPACT 📶

Likelihood x Impact provides a fast way to prioritize a list of items, by relatively comparing levels of how likely they are to happen and their impact.

RUNNING THE ACTIVITY:

1. Draw the Likelihood x Impact graph and place the items from the previous activity near it.
2. Ask participants to grade each item and place them in the graph, positioned accordingly:
   * What is the likelihood of this happening? Low, medium or high?
   * In case it does happen, what is the impact? Low, medium or high?
3. Identify the top ranked items (high likelihood, high impact) as the ones that will be tackled by the team.

This activity brings visibility to the highly likely and impactful items. These should take priority amongst all the items.

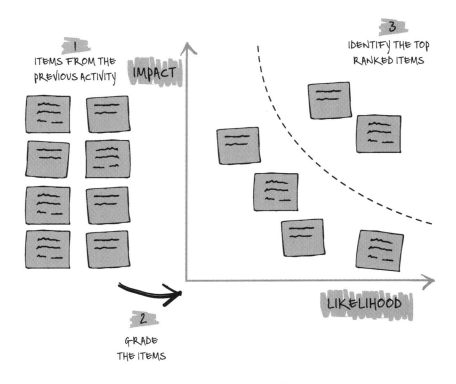

1

ITEMS FROM THE
PREVIOUS ACTIVITY

IMPACT

3

IDENTIFY THE TOP
RANKED ITEMS

LIKELIHOOD

2

GRADE
THE ITEMS

REMOTE-TEAM ADVICE: This activity works well for remote teams. Use a remote board that allows the input to be moved freely. After participants add their notes to the main course activity, ask them to move their notes to the graph area as they filter it.

EFFORT X VALUE 📶

Effort x Value provides a fast way to prioritize a list of items, by relatively comparing the effort to complete the item and how valuable it is.

RUNNING THE ACTIVITY:

1. Draw the Effort x Value graph and place the items from the previous activity near it.
2. Ask participants to grade each item and place them in the graph, positioned accordingly:
   * **Effort:** How much does it take to address this item?
   * **Value:** How much value will this bring?
3. Identify the top ranked items (low effort, high value) as the ones that will be tackled by the team.

This activity is inspired by Fabio Pereira's post on Technical Debt Wall Retrospective.[28] It is very effective for filtering out the items, prioritizing the ones with higher return.

[28] PEREIRA, Fabio. *Technical Debt Wall Retrospective*. Available at: <http://fabiopereira.me/blog/2009/09/01/technical-debt-retrospective/>. Access on: May, 2020.

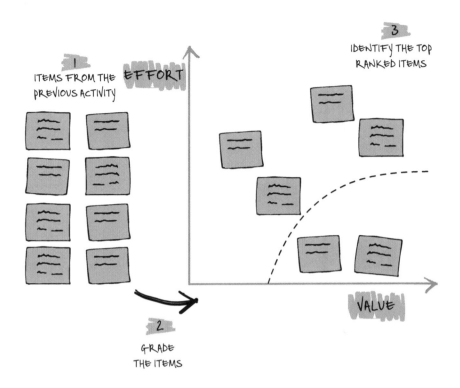

1
ITEMS FROM THE
PREVIOUS ACTIVITY

EFFORT

3
IDENTIFY THE TOP
RANKED ITEMS

VALUE

2
GRADE
THE ITEMS

REMOTE-TEAM ADVICE: This activity works well for remote teams. Use a remote board that allows the input to be moved freely. After participants add their notes to the main course activity, ask them to move their notes to the graph area as they filter it.

CHECK-OUT

A check-out activity happens right before participants depart from the meeting. It's typically focused on either <u>organizing action items</u> based on the previous conversation or <u>gathering information about the meeting itself:</u> how valuable it was, how much was learned, how worthy being at the meeting was, and any specific feedback.

WHO-WHAT-WHEN STEPS TO ACTION 📶

Who-What-When Steps to Action helps define commitments and follow-up actions on meetings. Many meetings end with an unclear "next steps" or "action items" discussion. This activity avoids creating a list of tasks that are often handed out to possibly unwilling participants with no particular deadline attached.

RUNNING THE ACTIVITY:

1. Create a table structure that outlines WHO / WHAT / WHEN as column titles.
2. Ask participants to select (from previous activity) or write down a concrete step to which they can commit. These should be either (1) steps they are required to follow, or (2) steps they feel really strong about.
3. Each selected concrete step will form a row on the Who-What-When table. Ask participants to:
   * Place the sticky note with the step under the WHAT column.
   * Write the name of who is going to do the step in the WHO column.
   * Define WHEN the item will be done.

By focusing the discussion on a Who/What/When format, you can connect people with clear actions they have defined and committed to. It enables participants to be clear about their commitments and accountabilities, making visible to the whole group WHO is going to do WHAT by WHEN.

This activity is inspired in the Who/What/When Matrix game in the *Game Storming* book.

 **REMOTE-TEAM ADVICE**: This activity works well for remote teams. Use the tool of your choice to share and track the items.

FOLLOWING UP ON ACTION ITEMS 🛜

Following Up on Action Items is used for organizing an action item list. Lack of accountability for action items is a common complaint about retrospectives. This activity provides a simple and direct way to follow up on previously identified items.

RUNNING THE ACTIVITY:

1. Open the list of action items.
2. Add newly identified items.
3. Update the status for each item on the list.

    These are the possible status for the items on the list:

    * **Closed** – completed action items.
    * **Added** – newly added action items to the list.
    * **Pending** – things previously identified, but not completed yet.
    * **Dropped** – things that have been dropped. It clearly identifies an action item that has not been closed and will never be. Possible reasons: (1) the owner has left the team and no one else picked it up, or (2) the owner states that the item will not be worked upon and no one else decides to pick it up.

The sample table below shows a possible format for following up on action items.

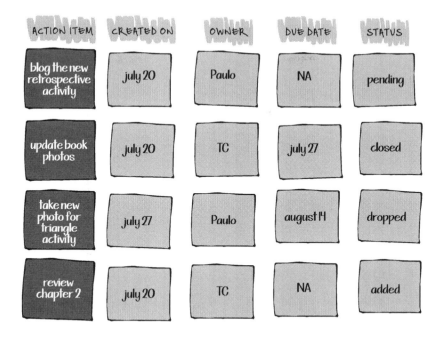

ACTION ITEM	CREATED ON	OWNER	DUE DATE	STATUS
blog the new retrospective activity	july 20	Paulo	NA	pending
update book photos	july 20	TC	july 27	closed
take new photo for triangle activity	july 27	Paulo	august 14	dropped
review chapter 2	july 20	TC	NA	added

Each team will have a different tool for tracking their action items. Some examples: sticky note on the team wall, a shared Excel document, Trello, Evernote.

Many teams have been following action items vigorously. Others have been complaining by not following it. Having this as a check-out activity and planned in the retrospective agenda acknowledges its importance. Although important, this should be used with caution, because of its inherent status reporting style.

REMOTE-TEAM ADVICE: This activity works well for remote teams. Use the tool of your choice to share and track the items.

SMART ITEMS 🛜

SMART Items helps a group of people give a second look at and adjust their action items to make them easier to understand and know when they should be done.

1. Pick-up one action item previously identified, discuss with the team, and take notes for each of the following:
   * **Specific** – define the specific area for improvement.
   * **Measurable** – determine a clear indicator of completion.
   * **Assignable** – specify who will do it.
   * **Realistic** – state which results can realistically be achieved.
   * **Time-bound** – specify when the result(s) can be achieved.
2. Repeat for all action items.

S.M.A.R.T. is an acronym created in 1981 by George T. Doran :

> *"There's a S.M.A.R.T. way to write management's goals and objectives."*[29]

It was originally used for giving criteria to guide the setting of management goals and objectives. But since its creation it has been widely used in many contexts, such as retrospective action items.

---

[29] DORAN, G. T. *There's a S.M.A.R.T. way to write management's goals and objectives.* Management Review (AMA FORUM) 70 (11): 35–36, 1981.

Typically, teams will struggle to complete action items that are not SMART. This activity helps better frame the items so they are accomplishable.

 **REMOTE-TEAM ADVICE:** This activity works well for remote teams. Use the tool of your choice to share and track the items.

FEEDBACK AND ROI 📶

Feedback and ROI (short for Return on Investment) is a great activity for closing a retrospective, a long meeting or an event.

RUNNING THE ACTIVITY:

1. Ask participants to write down on a sticky note a feedback about the retrospective/meeting/event.
2. Ask them to place the sticky note on the ROI (Return on Investment) radar. The ROI radar has a line going from very little ROI to very high ROI. You can represent the ROI as a "-" and "+" scale, sad and happy faces or a grading system.

   "For your time in this retrospective, how do you measure the return on your investment (of your time)? I am super-happy; this was really worth my time: goes on top; the opposite goes at the bottom."

It is always important to measure the return on investment of things we do. It is especially useful after a retrospective or workshop. Along with the ROI, this activity brings insights with feedback from participants.

The ROI in this activity is similar to NPS (Net Promoter Score).[30] You can change it so that you have a scale from 0 to 10 (the NPS) and the reason for it is the feedback on the sticky note.

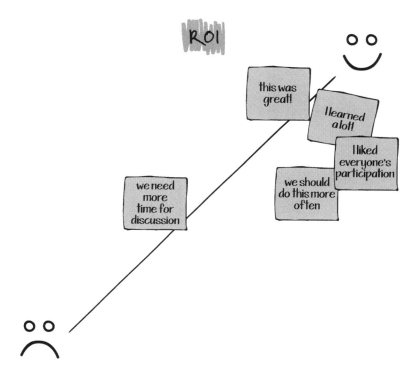

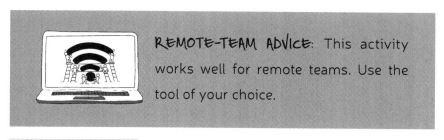

REMOTE-TEAM ADVICE: This activity works well for remote teams. Use the tool of your choice.

30 REICHHELD, Fred; MARKEY, Rob. *The Ultimate Question 2.0*. Harvard Business Review Press, 2011.

TOKEN OF APPRECIATION ≈

Token of Appreciation is great for fostering and acknowledging teamwork.

1. Ask people to form a circle.
2. You can start by saying: "I would like to acknowledge Paulo in recognition for that time when he helped me with…"
3. The person who received the recognition is the next one to appreciate someone.
4. Repeat as the time permits.

This is a great activity for acknowledgement, increasing the team morale and putting the team on a good mood. A tasty advice is to use a box of chocolates as a token of appreciation. Participants pass the box around and give a chocolate as they appreciate their colleagues. It works both as an opening and as a closing activity for a meeting.

REMOTE-TEAM ADVICE: This activity works well for remote teams. Use the communication tool of your choice.

LEARNING SCALE 📶

Learning Scale is a quick activity to measure how participants felt after attending a knowledge-sharing session, such as a presentation or training.

RUNNING THE ACTIVITY:

1. Draw a vertical line with five grades (from 1 to 5) on it and write the following sentence on top: "My grade as I enter this meeting."
2. When participants enter the room for the given session, ask them to select their place on a scale from 1 to 5, where 1 represents "I don't know anything about this subject," and 5 refers to "I consider myself an expert in this area."
3. After the session is done, draw a second vertical line with grades and the following sentence: 'My grade as I leave this meeting."
4. Ask participants to do the same, but in the second grading line.

Although this activity is not an accurate measure of how much participants effectively learned in that session, it shows how they felt about it. They may have been exposed to how much they still need to learn about that subject, or they may have learned something new and actually improved their knowledge.

LEARNING SCALE

my grade as
I enter ths
meeting

my grade as
I leave this
meeting

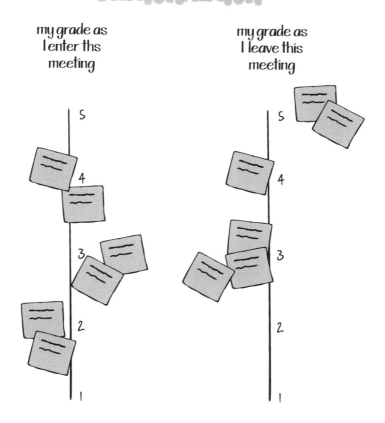

REMOTE-TEAM ADVICE: This activity works well for remote teams. Use a remote board of your choice.

NOTE TO SELF 🛜

Note to Self is a very simple check-out activity. It focuses on the self, without any commitments to the group. Therefore, it is a good option after group conversations without clear group action items.

RUNNING THE ACTIVITY:

1. Ask participants to grab a pen and a sticky note.
2. Give them one minute to reflect upon the discussion that has just ended.
3. Request each person to write a note to self about something they want to have and put on their laptop as a reminder for the future.

Though simple, writing a note and then reading it later on is a powerful way to have a person think and then ponder (again) on something. Reflections are very personal, and not everything needs to be a group discussion or group action items. We find the note to self very powerful for fostering individual thoughts and reflections.

 **REMOTE-TEAM ADVICE**: This activity works well for remote teams, as each participant writes their note individually and keeps it to themselves.

ONE WORD BEFORE LEAVING 📶

One Word Before Leaving is a check-out activity used to verify everyone's feelings before closing the retrospective. Typically, it is a great moment for people to share their feelings, especially when they have been very enthusiastic with the retrospective.

RUNNING THE ACTIVITY:

1. Ask them to describe their feelings (before they leave the room) in one word.

   "Please share with us in one word how you are feeling now, at the end of this retrospective."

2. Add the words to an open canvas.

3. Ask if someone wants to share more about their selected word.

This activity is very motivational, inspiring people to speak out loud about how they feel at the end of the retrospective. Typically, it gets highly motivated people to infect other participants right before closing the meeting.

ONE WORD BEFORE LEAVING

MOTIVATED

MOTIVATED

HAPPY

ENERGIZED

ANXIOUS

CALMER

REMOTE-TEAM ADVICE: This activity works well for remote teams. Use a remote board of your choice.

FUN PHOTO 📶

Fun Photo is an activity to collect a team memory for the future. Many times, a picture reminds us of a great moment. You should keep this memory. But, for that, you will want to put some fun into it!

RUNNING THE ACTIVITY:

1. Ask everyone to get ready for the photo (funny hat, crazy face, sticky note drawing on the forehead, anything!).
2. Take the photo.
3. Share it with the team or upload it somewhere to look at in the future.

Teams are made up of great memories. Something as simple as a photo can help with team morale and with lightening up the mood, getting everyone ready for the work ahead!

 REMOTE-TEAM ADVICE: This activity works well for remote teams. Take a screenshot from the video conference tool of your choice. Make sure all participants are visible.

THANKS FOR READING

We don't have time to do everything, so we make choices. The activities in this book get you there fast and effectively. And in a **fun** way! By following these activities and ideas, your team will increase the quality of their contributions. You'll have a good sense that the activities you use are successful when your team achieves insights it didn't have before.

The activities in this book allow groups to sort their ideas into relevant actions and pick the ones they think will have the highest immediate impact. Over time, your team will get so used to such activities that they will be following a continuous improvement culture. The high frequency of fun activities motivate and foster teamwork. Action items become proactive instead of reactive. Highly motivated, the team performs even better and gracefully attacks problems while they are still small.

Retrospectives are a wide area with ample literature about it, many options and techniques. While this book provides you with a versatile tool set with many ideas, we recommend you keep learning and improving, the same way we want our teams to!

Our journey with retrospectives presented us with many challenges and a lot of learning. We hope that, by sharing our experience with you throughout this book, we have helped you enable your team to be even more successful. Thank you for reading, and have fun in your next retrospective!

WHERE TO FIND MORE

You can find the activities described in this book, and more, at funretrospectives.com. We keep the site up-to-date with new activities as we discover, apply and validate them. Retrospectives are a wide area with ample literature about it, many options and techniques. While this book provides you with a versatile tool set with many ideas, we recommend you keep learning and improving, the same way we want our teams to!

Before you go, make sure to download the bonus content available at funretrospectives.com/bonus. On it, you will find a nice poster with the 7 step retrospective agenda, amongst other up-to-date infochart such as the most used activities combination (as per the FunRetrospectives website agenda builder).

JOIN THE FUNRETROSPECTIVES TRAINING

At first, we thought that just sharing activities with the community would be enough. As time went by, we realized that the personal interaction between facilitators, along with their sharing of experiences and ideas, is so valuable and yet so challenging to happen.

As such, we connected with more facilitators and communities and together we started organizing events and training material to share with everyone.

CHECK IT OUT!

www.caroli.org/en/training/funretrospectives/

TAINÃ CAETANO COIMBRA is a software engineer passionate about learning and continuous improvement, with over ten years of experience in the industry as a developer, coach, mentor, and facilitator. Having worked with multiple teams across Brazil, Asia, Europe and North America in his career, TC has found great value in fostering team dynamics that elevate all team members to be the best that they can be. TC has a Bachelor's Degree in Computer Science from the Federal University of Pelotas and works for Split Software.

FOLLOW THE AUTHOR AT:

in TAINACAETANO

PAULO CAROLI is passionate about innovation, entrepreneurship, and digital products. He is a software engineer, author, speaker, and successful facilitator.

Principal consultant at ThoughtWorks and cofounder of AgileBrazil, Paulo Caroli has over twenty years of experience in software development, working in various corporations in Brazil, India, USA, and in other countries of Latin America and Europe. In 2000, he discovered Extreme Programming and, since then, has focused his expertise in processes and practices of Agile & Lean. He joined ThoughtWorks in 2006 and has held the positions of Agile Coach, Trainer, Project Manager and Delivery Manager. Caroli has a Bachelor degree of Computer Science and a MS in Software Engineering, both from PUC-Rio.

He is the author, among other works, of the best-seller Lean Inception, which has been published in four languages.

FOLLOW THE AUTHOR AT:

WWW.CAROLI.ORG

 @PAULOCAROLI

 PAULOCAROLI

 PAULO.CAROLI

ABOUT EDITORA CAROLI

For readers and authors who seek and share knowledge in an agile way, Editora Caroli is a boutique publisher—all books are written, read, edited and/or revised by Paulo Caroli, who assists in the production, dissemination, and distribution of books and e-books. Unlike traditional publishers, Editora Caroli gives access to knowledge in its essence, making the text of new potential books available via free e-books, in addition to supporting events and educational institutions by presenting them with free published books.

At **www.caroli.org** you will find this and other quality content. Enjoy, as many e-books in WIP are available for free.

WIP (WRITING IN PROGRESS)

Editora Caroli has a different work method, bringing authors closer to their readers since the beginning of the content generation. Why wait for the author to finish writing to find out whether the content is good? In the current world, this does not make sense. For this reason, Editora Caroli promotes the sharing (free whenever possible) of WIP through e-book formats (pdf, mobi and epub). This way, readers have quick access to new ideas and can be part of the evolution of the work. For the authors, it is an effective form of feedback and motivation for content generation.

BEFORE YOU LEAVE A REVIEW

Thank you for buying and reading this book. If you have gotten this far, it means you've just finished it. Congratulations!

Authors live and die for the ratings they receive from readers. So, if you liked this book, we will be extremely happy to receive a five-star rating on your review.

If you have any feedback, please send an e-mail and tell us what to improve: contact@funretrospectives.com .

The biggest benefit of the e-book is the ease with which we can update content and correct any errors so that your reading experience gets better and better.

Thanks!

Printed in Great Britain
by Amazon

79999791R00139